Running Behavioral Studies

Participants

To our teachers, colleagues, students, and subjects who have taught us this material both explicitly and implicitly.

Running Behavioral Studies
With Human
Participants

A Practical Guide

FRANK E. RITTER
The Pennsylvania State University

JONG W. KIM
University of Central Florida

JONATHAN H. MORGAN
The Pennsylvania State University

RICHARD A. CARLSON
The Pennsylvania State University

Los Angeles | London | New Delhi
Singapore | Washington DC

Los Angeles | London | New Delhi
Singapore | Washington DC

FOR INFORMATION:

SAGE Publications, Inc.
2455 Teller Road
Thousand Oaks, California 91320
E-mail: order@sagepub.com

SAGE Publications Ltd.
1 Oliver's Yard
55 City Road
London EC1Y 1SP
United Kingdom

SAGE Publications India Pvt. Ltd.
B 1/I 1 Mohan Cooperative Industrial Area
Mathura Road, New Delhi 110 044
India

SAGE Publications Asia-Pacific Pte. Ltd.
3 Church Street
#10-04 Samsung Hub
Singapore 049483

Copyright © 2013 by SAGE Publications, Inc.

Printed in the United States of America

Library of Congress Cataloging-in-Publication Data

Running behavioral studies with human participants : a practical guide / Frank Ritter . . . [et al.].

p. cm.
Includes bibliographical references and index.

ISBN 978-1-4522-1742-0 (pbk.)

1. Human experimentation in psychology.
2. Psychology, Experimental.
3. Psychology—Research. I. Ritter, Frank E.

BF181.R86 2013
150.72'4—dc23   2012027003

This book is printed on acid-free paper.

Acquisitions Editor: Reid Hester
Editorial Assistant: Sarita Sarak
Production Editor: Laureen Gleason
Copy Editor: Megan Granger
Typesetter: C&M Digitals (P) Ltd.
Proofreader: Vicki Reed-Castro
Indexer: Karen Wiley
Cover Designer: Anupama Krishnan
Marketing Manager: Lisa Brown
Permissions Editor: Karen Ehrmann

SFI label applies to text stock

12 13 14 15 16 10 9 8 7 6 5 4 3 2 1

Brief Contents

Detailed Contents

List of Figures and Tables

Tables

Figures

Preface

There are few practical guides on how to prepare and run experiments with human participants in a laboratory setting. In our experience, we have found that students are taught how to design experiments and analyze data in courses such as Design of Experiments and Statistics. On the other hand, the dearth of materials available to students preparing and running experiments has often led to a gap between theory and practice in this area, which is particularly acute outside of psychology departments. Consequently, labs frequently must impart these practical skills to students informally.

This guide presents advice that can help young experimenters and research assistants run experiments more effectively and more comfortably with human participants. In this book, our purpose is to provide hands-on knowledge about and actual procedures for experiments. We hope this book will help students of psychology, engineering, and the sciences run studies with human participants in a laboratory setting. This will particularly help students (or instructors and researchers) who are not in large departments or who are running participants in departments that do not have a large or long history of experimental studies of human behavior. This book is also intended to help people who are starting to run user and usability studies in industry.

The book is an attempt to make the implicit knowledge in this area, "the just common sense" as one reviewer called it, be more explicit and more common. David Foster Wallace noted this effect in his retelling of a parable of how fish don't know they are in water.[1] The same effect happens in our field, where the knowledge of how to implement and run a study is often known implicitly, and thus it is hard to learn if you are outside of the community that uses that knowledge.

---

[1]We thank Josh Gross for pointing out this story to us.

We have addressed this book to advanced undergraduates and early graduate students starting to run experiments without previous experience, but we believe this guide will be useful to anyone who is starting to run research studies, training people to run studies, or studying the experimental process. It should also be useful to researchers in industry who are also starting to run studies.

We are generally speaking here from our background running cognitive psychology, cognitive ergonomics, and human–computer interaction studies. Because it is practical advice, we do not cover experimental design or data analyses. This practical advice will be less applicable in more distant areas, or when working in more complex situations, but may still be of use. For example, we do not cover how to use complex apparatus, such as functional magnetic resonance imaging (fMRI) or event-related potential (ERP). We also do not cover field studies or studies that in the United States require a full a review by an Institutional Review Board (IRB). This means that we do not cover how to work with unusual populations such as prisoners, animals, and children, or how to take and use measures that include risks to the subjects or experimenter (e.g., saliva, blood samples, or private information).

This book arose during a discussion at Jong Kim's PhD graduation. Ritter asked Kim where he thought more training might have been helpful; the conversation turned to experimental methods and the tactics and details of running studies. During the graduation ceremony, they outlined this book—a worthy genesis for a book, we think. Since then, we and others have used it to teach both in classrooms and as conference tutorials, and it has been expanded, corrected, and extended.

When running an experiment, ensuring its repeatability is of greatest importance—addressing variations in either method or participant behavior is critical. Running an experiment in exactly the same way regardless of who is conducting it or where (e.g., different research teams or laboratories) is essential. In addition, reducing unanticipated variance in the participants' behavior is key to an experiment's repeatability. This book will help you achieve these requirements, increasing both your comfort and that of the participants in your experiments.

This book consists of several sections, with multiple appendices. As an advance organizer, we briefly describe each section's contents.

Chapter 1, Introduction, provides an overview of the research process and describes where experiments and controlled observation fit into the research process. If you have taken either an experimental methods course or a research design course, you can skip this chapter. If, on the other hand, you are either a new research assistant or working on a project in which you are unclear of your role or how to proceed, this chapter may provide some helpful context. This chapter also introduces several running examples.

Chapter 2, Preparation for Running Experiments, describes pertinent topics for preparing to run your experiment—such as supplemental reading materials, recruitment of participants, choosing experimental measures, and getting IRB approval for experiments involving participants.

Chapter 3, Potential Ethical Problems, describes ethical considerations necessary for safely running experiments with human participants—that is, how to ethically recruit participants, how to handle data gathered from participants, how to use that data, and how to report that data. Being vigilant and aware of these topics is an important component to rigorous, as well as ethical, research.

Chapter 4, Risks to Validity to Avoid While Running an Experiment, describes risks that can invalidate your experimental data. If you fail to avoid these types of risks, you may obtain either false or uninterpretable results from your study. Thus, before starting your study, you should be aware of these risks and how to avoid them.

Chapter 5, Running a Research Session, describes practical information about what you have to do when you run a research session. This section will give an example procedure that you can follow.

Chapter 6, Concluding a Study, describes practical information about what to do at the conclusion of each experimental session and at the end of a study.

The **Afterword** briefly summarizes the book and describes the appendices.

The **Appendices** include an example checklist for preparing a study, a checklist for setting up a study, an example consent form, an example debriefing form, and an example IRB form. The details and formats of these forms will vary by lab and IRB committee, but the materials in the appendices provide examples of the style and tone. There is also an appendix on how this material could apply to online studies.

A website holding supplementary material is available at www .frankritter.com/rbs/.

Acknowledgments

Crhristine Cardone at SAGE provided some encouragement when we needed it, and the production team at SAGE has been very helpful and has greatly improved this book. Numerous people have given useful comments, and when they have used it in teaching we note that here as well. Ray Adams (Middlesex), Michelle Ahrens, Susanne Bahr (Florida Institute of Technology, who suggested the figures at the start of each chapter), Ellen Bass, Gordon Baxter (St. Andrews), Stephen Broomell, Karen Feigh (Georgia Institute of Technology, several times), Katherine Hamilton, William (Bill) Kennedy, Alex Kirlik (U. of Illinois), Michelle Moon, Geoffrey Morgan (CMU), Razvan Orendovici, Erika Poole, Michael (Q) Qin (NSMRL/U. of Connecticut), Joseph Sanford, Robert West (Carleton), Hongbin Wong (U. of Texas/Houston), Kuo-Chuan (Martin) Yeh, Xiaolong (Luke) Zhang (PSU), and several anonymous reviewers have provided useful comments. Ryan Moser and Joseph Sanford in the ACS Lab at Penn State have helped prepare this manuscript. Any incompleteness or inadequacies remain the fault of the authors.

Preparation of this manuscript was partially sponsored by a grant from the Division of Human Performance Training and Education at the Office of Naval Research, under Contracts W911QY-07-01-0004 and N00014-11-1-0275. The views and conclusions contained in this report are those of the authors and should not be interpreted as representing the official policies, either expressed or implied, of the U.S. Government or The Pennsylvania State University.

About the Authors

Frank E. Ritter is a professor of information sciences and technology, of psychology, and of computer science and engineering at Penn State. He researches the development, application, and methodology of cognitive models—particularly as applied to interface design, predicting the effect of behavioral moderators, and understanding learning—and conducts experiments to test these models. With Martin Yeh, he has developed a popular iPhone app, CaffeineZone, for predicting the time course and effects of caffeine. His lab is building and testing tutors on several topics. His report on applying cognitive models in synthetic environments was published by the Human Systems Information Analysis Center as a State of the Art Report (2003). His book on order effects on learning was published in 2007 by Oxford, and he contributed to a National Research Council report on how to use cognitive models to improve human-system design (Pew & Mavor, 2007). He is working on a textbook addressing the ABCs of the psychology that systems designers need to know (to be published by Springer), which has repeatedly won awards at the Human–Computer Interaction Consortium's annual meeting.

His papers on modeling have won awards; one on high-level languages, with St. Amant, was selected for the "Siegel-Wolf Award for Best Applied Modeling Paper" at the International Conference on Cognitive Modeling, and four have won awards at the Behavior Representation in Modeling and Simulation Conference. He currently edits the Oxford Series on Cognitive Models and Architectures for Oxford University Press. He serves on the editorial boards of *Cognitive Systems Research, Human Factors,* and *IEEE SMC, Part A: Systems and Humans.*

Jong W. Kim is a research faculty member in the Department of Psychology at the University of Central Florida. He received his PhD in the Department of Industrial Engineering at the Pennsylvania State University. His academic pursuit is to improve cognitive systems supporting optimized user performance. To that end, he runs experiments with human subjects and models human cognition. His recent research, sponsored by the Office of Naval Research, has investigated skill learning and forgetting, and he has developed a theory of skill retention that is being applied to a couple of intelligent tutoring systems. His current research projects focus on the influence of affect on the three stages of learning by an understanding of non-vocal expressions. Particularly, he is interested in helping autistic children learn social communication skills with human-centered computer systems.

Jonathan H. Morgan is a research assistant and lab manager for Penn State's Applied Cognitive Science Lab, where he manages people running studies about learning, retention, and usability. Morgan has published in *Computational and Mathematical Organization Theory*, received two paper awards from the Behavior Representation in Modeling and Simulation conference committee, and coauthored papers published in the proceedings of the annual conference of the Cognitive Science Society, the International Conference on Cognitive Modeling, and the annual conference of the Biologically Inspired Cognitive Architectures Society. He has also contributed to the design, development, and testing of two tutors. His current research includes modeling socio-cognitive processes and examining the acquisition of procedural knowledge in complex tasks.

Richard A. Carlson is professor of psychology at Penn State University, where he has been on the faculty for 27 years. He received his BSS from Cornell College and his PhD from the University of Illinois. He conducts experiments examining cognitive control, cognitive skill, and conscious awareness, focusing on control at the time scale of 1 second or less. Previous research has addressed topics such as causal thinking, the development of troubleshooting skill, task switching, the role of gesture in mental arithmetic, and the structure of conscious intentions. Current research projects focus on the role of affect in working memory and cognitive control, the effect of cognitive workload on metacognition, and changes in metacognition with increasing skill. He has published in journals such as *Journal of Experimental Psychology: Learning, Memory, and Cognition; Memory & Cognition;* and *Human Factors*. His book, *Experienced Cognition* (1998), which describes a theory of consciousness and cognitive skill, won a CHOICE Outstanding Academic Book award.

Professor Carlson currently serves as associate head and director of Undergraduate Studies in Penn State's Department of Psychology. He is the founding coordinator of the department's online psychology major. In 2009, he received an Outstanding Faculty Adviser award. He serves on the editorial boards of the *Journal of Experimental Psychology: Learning, Memory, and Cognition; Behavior Research Methods;* and the *American Journal of Psychology*. He is a fellow of the American Psychological Association. His website is psych.la.psu.edu/directory/faculty-bios/carlson.html.

1

Introduction

Individuals who conduct behavioral research with human participants as part of their jobs, like other specialists, have developed a set of good practices, standard methodology, and specialized vocabulary for discussing the research process. If you have taken a course in research methods or read a standard research methods textbook, much of this vocabulary will be familiar to you. We assume, however, that many readers of this book are new to research or will find some reminders useful. If you are new, the practical techniques learned through a hands-on apprenticeship might not be available to you in your situation, and providing that knowledge is the purpose of this book.

We focus here on behavioral research, by which we mean research with the primary object of observing, understanding, and predicting behavior. These actions can be primarily physical, but behavioral research is typically concerned with the meaning of behavior—the answers communicated by speech, key presses, or other means; the effect of actions in achieving goals; and so on. Behavioral research is often contrasted with neuroscience research, which is primarily concerned with understanding how the brain and nervous system support behavior. Much of what we have to say is drawn from the field of experimental psychology, but researchers in many fields make use of behavioral research methods.

1.1 Background

This book is primarily about conducting *experiments*. In everyday usage, *experimenting* simply means trying something out—a new recipe, a different word-processing program, or perhaps a new exercise routine. In this book, however, *experiment* has a more formal definition. That definition has two primary elements. First, we are concerned with *control*—not controlling our participants, though we'll sometimes want to do some of that, but controlling the circumstances under which we make our observations. Second, we are concerned with *cause and effect*, or the relationship between an *independent variable* and a *dependent variable*. Winston (1990) traced this use of the term *experiment* in psychology to Woodworth's (1938) classic text, which is perhaps the most influential book on methodology in the history of experimental psychology.

The concept of control is important because, more or less, almost everything affects almost everything else in an experimental situation. For example, if we are interested in whether people prefer a new computer interface, we have to recognize that their reactions may be influenced by their mood, the time of day, extraneous noises, their familiarity with similar interfaces, and so on. Much of this book is about how researchers can achieve control of the circumstances under which they make their observations. Sometimes this is done by actually controlling the circumstances—making our observations at consistent times of day or eliminating extraneous noises. Sometimes, it is done using statistical methods to account for factors we cannot literally control. These statistical methods are also referred to as *control*.

Sometimes, controlling the conditions of our observations is sufficient to answer a research question. If we simply want to know whether individuals find an interface pleasant to work with, we can ask them to use the interface under controlled conditions and assess their reactions through interviews or rating schemes. This is called controlled observation. If controlled observation is sufficient for your research purpose, you will still find much useful advice in this book about how to achieve control. Much of product development uses these types of studies, and a lot can be learned in this way about how people use technology. More often, though, observations such as this raise the question, "Compared with what?"

In contrast to controlled observation, an experiment—sometimes called a "true experiment"—involves manipulating an independent variable. For example, our question might not be whether individuals find an interface pleasant to work with but whether they find Interface A more pleasant than Interface B, or vice versa. In this case, the independent variable would be the interface, and the variable would have two levels, A and B. The dependent variable would be whatever we measure—users' ratings, their success in using the interface, and so on. A true experiment has at least one independent and one dependent variable but can have more than one of both. Independent variables are also sometimes called *factors*.

It is important to know some of the other jargon common to a psychology laboratory. A *stimulus* is an environmental event—typically, now, a display on a computer screen—to which a subject *responds*. Most experiments involve numerous *trials*—individual episodes in which a stimulus is displayed and a response measured. Often, these trials are grouped into *blocks* to provide sets of observations that serve as units of analysis, or to mark events in the experimental procedure such as rest periods for subjects. The language of *stimulus, response, trial,* and *block* is often awkward for experiments using complex, dynamic tasks. Nevertheless, these terms are used frequently enough in the field and in this book that they should become familiar. The terms we have introduced here, and others that will be useful in reading this book, are briefly defined in Table 1.1.

We will also frequently mention "the literature" relevant to an experiment. This simply means the accumulated articles, chapters, and books that report related research. Reading relevant scientific literature is important because it can help sharpen your research question, allow you to avoid mistakes, and deepen your understanding of the results. University libraries generally have powerful database tools for searching for research related to a particular topic. Common databases are PsycInfo (a very complete database maintained by the American Psychological Association) and Web of Science (a database allowing citation searches, provided by Thomson Reuters). CiteSeer, Google Scholar, and PubMed also offer access to databases of papers, but their coverage is not as broad in this area.

The trick to searching the literature using these databases is to know the appropriate keywords. For many researchers conducting experiments for the first time, this can be an obstacle. For example, understanding how individuals use an interface may, depending on the specific question, lead to issues relating to working memory, attention, perception, skill, or motor control. Each of these domains of cognitive research has generated a vast literature. Sometimes, reading a handful of abstracts found with a database search will help focus the search.

Another resource for many topics is online references such as Wikipedia, but you should be aware that Wikipedia articles provide only starting points and are not considered primary resources because they are not fully reviewed (someone has checked them) or archival (copies are kept), and change over time. Often, the best strategy is to find a friendly expert, tell him or her about your research question, and ask for suggestions on what to read. We will return to the topic of reading the relevant literature in Chapter 2.

With this as background, we turn to an overview of the research process.

Table 1.1. Definitions.

Block: A portion of an experiment distinguished by breaks for subjects, shifts in procedure, and so on. Typically, a block is a set of trials. Often, blocks serve as units of analysis.

Condition (experimental condition): A subset of the experiment defined by a level or value of an independent variable.

Control: The holding constant by procedure or statistical procedure of variables other than the independent variable.

Controlled observation: Observing behavior in a situation that is relatively constant across subjects.

Dependent variable (DV): A variable that depends on the subjects' behavior, such as the time to respond or the accuracy of the response.

Experiment: A study in which an independent variable is manipulated, a dependent variable measured, and other variables controlled.

Experimenter (E): A member of the research team who interacts directly with subjects. The experimenter may be one of the researchers, or someone whose sole role is interacting with subjects to carry out experimental procedures.

Hypothesis: A prediction about the outcome of an experiment, stated as an expected relationship between the independent and dependent variables.

Independent variable (IV): A variable that is manipulated by the researcher. The values of an independent variable are independent of the subjects' behavior.

Informed consent: The process by which subjects are first informed about what they will experience if they participate in the study and, second, indicate whether they consent to take part.

Institutional Review Board (IRB): The panel responsible for reviewing experimental procedures for compliance with ethical and regulatory standards.

Investigator, principal investigator (PI), researcher, lead researcher: The individuals responsible for making scientific decisions and judgments. *Principal investigator* refers to the individual who takes final responsibility for the study to granting agencies, the IRB, etc. *Lead researcher* refers to the individual who designs and makes scientific judgments about the study. In practice, although the principal investigator role is usually officially defined, the distinctions among roles may be blurred.

Null hypothesis: The hypothesis in which the independent variable does not affect the dependent variable. The null hypothesis serves a special role in tests of statistical significance. For example, a null hypothesis is that two interfaces have an equal error rate and the same user satisfaction rating.

Pilot: To test aspects of a study before running a formal study
Power: The power in an experimental study indicates the probability that the test (or experiment) will reject a false null hypothesis.
Response: The units of the subjects' behavior. Responses may be key presses, verbal answers, moves in a problem environment, and so on.
Statistical power: The ability or sensitivity of an experiment to detect an effect of an independent variable
Statistical significance: A criterion for deciding that the experimental hypothesis is sufficiently more likely than the null hypothesis to allow the conclusion that the independent variable affects the dependent variable; also called statistical reliability to separate repeatability from importance
Stimulus: An environmental event to which a subject responds
Subject or participant (S or P): An individual who performs the experimental task and whose behavior is the object of analysis
Trial: An episode within an experiment in which a stimulus occurs and the subject responds

1.2 Overview of the Research Process

Figure 1.1 summarizes the research process, with notes about where in the book the step is discussed. A glance at the figure shows that the process is iterative—rarely do even experienced researchers generate an experiment without pilot testing. The dashed lines show loops that sometimes occur, and the solid line shows the main loop. Piloting almost always results in the refinement of the initial procedure.

The figure also shows that the process generally involves others—both other colleagues in your lab and outside institutions. Further, research with human subjects conducted in a university or other organization that receives federal funding (in the United States) requires the approval of an Institutional Review Board (IRB). An IRB evaluates the experimental procedure for possible risks to the participants and other ethical concerns, such as potential conflicts of interest. Other organizations and countries often have similar requirements. We return to the issue of ethics and IRB review in Chapters 2 and 3; for now, the point is that planning an experiment is almost always iterative and requires consultation with groups outside of the research team.

1. Identify the research problem and priorities, design the experiment. If you are planning to conduct research, you most likely already have a research topic

Figure 1.1.   A pictorial summary of the research process. This is similar to but developed separately from Bethel and Murphy's (2010) figure describing the process for human–robotic studies.

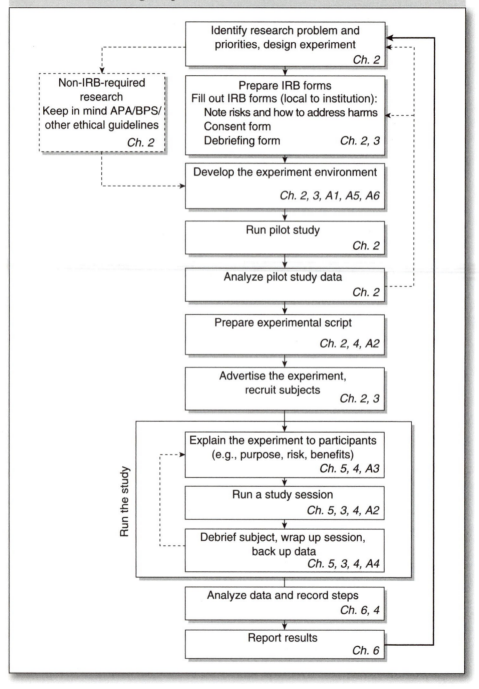

or question in mind. It is important, however, to clarify the research question in such a way as to provide a framework for developing an effective experiment. Typically, this process entails specifying one or more *hypotheses*—predictions about how one factor affects another. The hypothesis for a true experiment can be stated as a prediction that stipulates that changing the independent variable will cause changes in the dependent variable. For example, you might hypothesize that changing the amount of time subjects practice using an interface will affect how successfully they accomplish tasks with that interface. More specifically, it is important to predict the direction of that change if possible. In this case, we predict that *more* practice will result in *more* successful performance. Predicting the relationship is even better.

It is also important to consider how you will manipulate the independent variable. Exactly what will you change? How will you measure the dependent variable; and, what, specifically, counts as better performance? Answering these questions is sometimes called *operationalizing* or developing the *operational definitions* of your variables, because you are specifying the operations you will use to manipulate or measure them.

Sometimes, your research question may simply be, "I wonder what will happen if . . ." or "How do people like/use my new interface?" These relatively open-ended research questions are occasionally referred to as fishing expeditions, because you do not know what you will catch; the studies assume that gathering data will provide more insights. The studies can also be called controlled observation, because you would like the people being studied to interact with the interface in the same controlled circumstances. This type of question is sometimes criticized for being too general, but for exploratory work, it can be very successful. For example, one of the authors was part of a research team that suspected that subjects confronted with a problem would choose problem strategies based on certain features, but we did not know which features factored into the subjects' choices. So they included multiple types of problems and multiple types of features. Then, with analysis, they were able to pull out which features subjects relied on most often, based on their decisions across a wide range of problem types (Reder & Ritter, 1992).

This book does not describe how to design experiments. These steps are informed by numerous books on experimental design (some are listed at the end of this chapter). The book also does not explain how to analyze the data, for which, again, there are many excellent books available—some of which are noted in the further resources section.

2. Develop the experimental task and environment. While it is sometimes interesting to watch what people do when they are left to their own devices, an experiment generally involves giving subjects a specific task: classify these words, solve this problem, answer these questions, and so on. This is even true with controlled observation of a new interface, because the test users often have no prior familiarity with the interface.

It is important to carefully develop the task you will give your subjects and to design the environment in which they will perform the task. This development is often done in parallel and interacts with the whole experiment. For example, suppose you want to know how the spacing of learning—whether learning trials are massed into a single session or distributed over time—affects the ability to retain foreign vocabulary words. To set up this experiment, you would need lists of appropriate words, a means of displaying them, and a way to record the participants' responses.

Providing a task is typically done with a computer, often programmed using software packages, such as EPrime (Psychology Software Tools, Pittsburgh), specifically designed for behavioral experiments. To set up the vocabulary learning experiment, for example, you would also need to make a large number of practical decisions—how long to display words, how to test memory, and so on. It is especially important to think carefully about how you will collect your data and how you will verify that your data are being collected correctly. It is very frustrating to spend many hours running an experiment only to realize that the data were recorded incorrectly (ask us how we know!).

3. Evaluate potential ethical issues and seek human subjects (IRB) approval. Once your research protocol is fairly clear, you will want to evaluate your study plan for potential risks or other ethical concerns (e.g., whether your experiment examines differences in behavior as a consequence of limited or misinformation). After carefully considering these risks and strategies to mitigate them, you will be ready to seek approval from your organization's IRB, or human subjects panel, for running human subjects. You should be aware that such approval typically requires extensive paperwork and may take weeks for processing, so you should begin the process as soon as possible and schedule this time in your research agenda. The things you should consider—and that the IRB will want to know—include how you will recruit and compensate subjects, what you will tell them, whether any personal information will be collected, what they will be doing during your study, what risks subjects might incur by participating, how the data will be kept secure, and so on. Even if you are in a situation in which IRB approval is not required, it is important to think through these issues and plan in advance to address them. We will explain this in more detail in a later chapter.

4. Pilot test your procedure. A pilot test or pilot study is a preliminary experiment, usually with a small number of subjects, intended to let you test the design and procedure of your experiment before you make the investment required to run many subjects. It is an opportunity to make sure that the software running your study works correctly and that subjects understand the instructions (if there is a way to crash the software or to misinterpret the instructions, rest assured some subject will find it!). You may find that you need to adjust the design or procedure of your study. It is hard to overemphasize the importance of adequate pilot testing. It can be frustrating to take this time when you really want to get on to your "real" experiment, but you will save time and get better results in the long run.

Pilot testing often equates to recruiting whoever is convenient to try out your experiment. For example, you might ask friends and colleagues to try a mirror-tracing task. You might run people casually, in their offices, and record their times to learn how response times differ by stimuli. You would not report these results but, rather, would use them to make adjustments. For instance, you may need to alter your apparatus (perhaps adjusting the mirror), your stimuli (you might find how long it takes to follow each pattern), or your procedure (you might learn that you have to remind your participants multiple times not to look directly at the sheet of paper).

You will also want to analyze the data you collect during pilot testing. This analysis serves several purposes. First, you will learn whether you have collected data in a format that facilitates analysis, and whether there are any logical gaps between your experiment's design and your plan for analysis. Second, although you won't have a lot of statistical power (because you will have relatively little data), you will get a sense of whether your independent variable "works"—does it actually affect your dependent variable? Is the relationship in the direction you hypothesized (or at least in a direction you can interpret)? Finally, you may discover the "edge" of the formal or informal theory guiding your thinking. If, for instance, you are unable to interpret your pilot results using that theory, you may want to consider adjusting the direction of your research. Significant changes require notifying your IRB if you have submitted a proposal at this point.

5. Prepare an experimental script. During pilot testing, you will likely try various ways of instructing your subjects, as well as some variations to the procedure of your experiment. In your actual experiment, you will want both the manner of instruction and the procedure used to be consistent to ensure good experimental control. The best way to achieve this is to develop a script for the experimenter(s) running the study to follow. Like a script for a movie or play, this will specify the exact steps to be taken and their sequence. For critical portions, you may want to give your experimenters specific "lines"—instructions that are to be read verbatim to subjects to avoid inadvertently leaving things out or saying them in ways that can be interpreted differently. Again, significant changes require IRB notification and approval.

6. Advertise the experiment and recruit subjects. Sometimes recruiting subjects is easy, and sometimes recruiting is hard. It depends on your local circumstances, the study, and requirements for being a subject. If you have access to a subject pool, it is easier. If, on the other hand, your study requires particular subjects with particular expertise (such as airplane pilots), recruiting can be much harder.

Recruiting subjects can start while piloting and setting up the study, particularly if preparing the study is relatively easy or recruiting subjects is more difficult. On the other hand, if subjects are easy to recruit and the study is harder to prepare, then recruiting should probably occur after piloting the experiment.

7. Run the experiment. This is, of course, the heart of the process. In each session, subjects give informed consent, receive instructions, complete your experimental procedure, and are compensated and perhaps debriefed.

Running the experiment may result in different results from those of your pilot study. The primary cause for these differences is generally due to individual variability—participants may think or react in unanticipated ways. Or you may get different results because your study is more formal. In either of these cases or when there are fewer surprises, you are interested in seeing the truth about the world based on examining a sample of it. How to run the study is the focus of this book.

8. Analyze the results and archive your study. This is the payoff! If the pilot testing successfully verified the data collection and analysis strategy and the experiment's execution went as planned, you are ready to find out the answer to—or at least better understand—your research question by analyzing the data. The details of data analysis are beyond the scope of this book, but we can offer a few important points that arise while running the experiment.

First, back up your data! If they are on a computer disk, make a copy (or several copies). If they are on paper, photocopy them. Second, make sure the data are stored securely, both to ensure they are retained for use and that they remain confidential. Third, make sure that everything about your experiment is recorded and stored. This task includes archiving a copy of the program that presented materials and collected responses (it's no fun trying to figure out months later which of five similarly named files was actually used), a copy of the experimental script, a description of when and where the data were collected, and so on. You may think you'll remember all these details or that some are not important, but we know from experience that taking the time to carefully archive your study is worth it because data from an experiment can be used multiple times and much later than they were gathered (e.g., over a decade, this data set was analyzed multiple ways: Delaney, Reder, Staszewski, & Ritter, 1998; Heathcote, Brown, & Mewhort, 2000; Reder & Ritter, 1988, 1992; Ritter, 1989).

9. Rinse and repeat. Very often—in fact, almost always—your initial experiment is not sufficient to answer your research question. Your data may raise additional questions best addressed by a modification to your procedure or by evaluating the influence of an additional independent or dependent variable. Though not always necessary, conducting additional experiments is often important for understanding your results. Especially if your results are surprising, you may want to exactly repeat the experiment, or part of it, to make sure your results can be replicated.

10. Report your results. In this step, you take the results and prepare a manuscript. The form used for your manuscript will vary depending on your research goals. You may prepare a technical report for a sponsor, a conference paper to test your ideas by exposing them to fellow researchers, a journal article to disseminate novel insights gleaned from your experiment or experiments, or perhaps a thesis to examine a research idea or ideas within a broader context. Regardless of the type of manuscript, you will usually have help and guidance throughout this step (a few resources are noted at the end of this chapter). In addition, there are useful books on the details of the preparation (i.e., *Publication Manual of the American Psychology Association*). This step is worth keeping in mind throughout the experimental process, because reporting your data is not only what you are working toward but also the step that defines many of the requirements associated with the rest of the process (e.g., the emphasis on repeatability).

We have described here an idealized process. The description is normative, in that it specifies what should happen, especially for an inexperienced investigator starting from scratch. In practice, this process often runs in parallel, can vary in order (insights do not always come before or between experiments), and is iterative. Furthermore, breakthroughs frequently result from interactions between researchers across multiple experiments in a lab, so it is usually not a solitary activity.

1.3 Overview of the Running Examples

We introduce three examples we will use throughout the course of this book. These examples are hypothetical but in many cases draw from ongoing or published research. Not all examples will be used in all chapters, but we will use them to illustrate and extend points made in each chapter.

The experimental process begins with the question, "*What do we want to know?*" After determining what we want to know, we must then consider how we go about finding it out. This process entails framing the experiment into either a single falsifiable hypothesis or set of falsifiable hypotheses, or, in more complex or emergent situations, simply areas and behaviors where you want to know more. These areas influence the hypotheses, methods, and materials, so it is useful to consider several types of examples.

In the first example, we examine a study from the perspective of a principle investigator working with a special population. We follow Judy, a scientist for an R&D (research and development) company that cares about usability. The company specializes in on-demand streaming video. Judy's company is interested in making web-based media more accessible to partially sighted users—those users ranging from total blindness to vision correctable only to 20/70. Consequently, she is interested in improving web navigation for users dependent on screen readers, devices that provide audio descriptions of graphical interfaces. To generate this description, screen readers read the HTML tags associated with the page in question. Consequently, blind users who encounter navigation bars frequently must endure long lists of links. Past solutions have allowed users to skip to the first non-link line; however, Judy is interested in whether marking the navigation bar as a navigation feature that can be skipped unless specifically requested will improve web navigation for users dependent on screen readers.

Judy's outputs will range from short summaries of results for engineers to more formal technical reports summarizing the whole study and its results. The longer reports may be necessary to describe the context and relatively complex results.

In our second example, we examine a study from the perspective of a graduate student working with an undergraduate. It examines issues in managing less-experienced research assistants and the role of running studies as preparation for writing about them. We will meet Edward and Ying, students at a university. Edward has only recently joined a lab working with e-readers[1] and computer-assisted learning tools, while Ying is a PhD candidate in the lab working on an inexpensive laptop project on a small grant. As the manufacturer of the inexpensive laptop has looked to expand its outreach efforts in the Middle East and Asia, the project has found that common rectangular resolutions produce fuzzy, indistinct characters when displaying either Arabic or Hangul. Edward and Ying will be investigating the effects of different screen formats on readability of non-Roman alphabets. This research is one

---

[1]This example draws from Al-Harkan and Ramadan (2005) and Yeh, Gregory, and Ritter (2010).

component of Ying's thesis examining computer-assisted language learning. Edward will be helping Ying run subjects in experiments comparing three matrix formats. These formats will differ with respect to pixel density, size, and color. While the experiments are computer-based tests and surveys, Edward will be responsible for greeting participants, explaining the experiments, assisting the participants where necessary and appropriate, and ensuring that the tests have, in fact, successfully recorded the participants' results. To help Edward successfully complete these tasks, Ying will be working with Edward closely.

Ying, Edward, and their faculty advisor will want to report and get feedback on their work continually. How and where they do this informs and can shape the research process, including the details. This process can start with posters at conferences, which provide them with useful feedback and can help document results. Conference papers (in cognitive science and human–computer interaction [HCI]) provide larger ways to document work and result in more serious feedback. They will also be interested in Ying's PhD thesis and journal articles on the study.

Our final example focuses on a study done in industry, with incremental design as its goal. In this example, we will meet Bob, a human factors engineer, working for a medium-sized company getting into robotics. Bob is simply trying to improve his company's robot in whatever way he can. The platform is hard to change, while also still in flux due to changes being made by the hardware engineers. Bob's situation is the least likely to result in a classic study testing one or more hypotheses. Nevertheless, whether through a study, reading, or controlled observations, he can apply what he learns to improve the human–robot interface (HRI).

In addition, the outputs Bob will be preparing will vary more than for the other researchers. If his engineers are sympathetic and he has learned just a tidbit, he will be able to report what he learns with a simple e-mail that suggests a change (see, for example, Nielsen's comments on types of usability reports used in industry, at www.useit.com/alertbox/20050425.html). If his engineers are less sympathetic, or when he needs to report more details to suggest larger and more expensive changes, Bob will be preparing reports of usability studies, similar to a technical report. When or if he has general lessons for his field, he may prepare a conference paper or a journal article.

Table 1.2 presents the example studies and where they appear in the book, along with what the examples will cover. These studies will be used to provide working examples and to explore concepts. For example, hypotheses across these studies share some important characteristics: They are usually falsifiable (except in the controlled observation study), and they possess both independent and dependent variables. In Examples 1 and 2, there are clear *null* hypotheses: (1) Marking the navigation bar to be skipped unless requested *does not help* partially sighted users, and (2) manipulating pixel density, size, and color results *in no difference* in readability.

Each hypothesis also has independent and dependent variables. In the first example, a marked or unmarked navigation bar is the independent variable, while lag times both within and between the web pages are the dependent variable. For the second example, the independent variables are changes in pixel density, size, and color, while the dependent variables are user response times, number of correct responses, and preference rankings. In the third example, the hypotheses are not yet defined. In this case, Bob would be advised to generate some hypotheses, but his environment may allow him only to learn from controlled observation.

Once framed, a study's goals (the testing of a hypothesis, the detection or confirmation of a trend, or the identification of underlying relationships,

Table 1.2. Summary of example studies used across chapters.

Chapters	Low Vision HCI Study (primary investigator)	Multilingual Fonts Study (inexperienced RA working with graduate student)	HRI Study (engineer)
Ch. 2 Preparing the study	Recruiting/special prep	—	Piloting
Ch. 3 Ethics	Stress and compensation	Ethics and teamwork	—
Ch. 4 Risks to validity	—	Internal validity	External validity
Ch. 5 Running the study	Learning from piloting about apparatus and people	Learning from piloting about people and task	Subject recruitment and when to end the study
Ch. 6 Concluding a study	Findings and report	Debriefing Ss, writing up results	Format for reporting, archiving data
Publication goals	Proof of concept, technical report	Poster, conference paper, PhD thesis	Product changes and future products, technical report

etc.) inform the rest of the experimental process—all the steps in Figure 1.1. We discuss each step in greater detail in the remainder of the book. We will also map this process through our examples. At the end of each section, we will revisit these examples to demonstrate how the information presented in the section translates into practice.

1.4 Further Readings

A course in experimental methods is probably the best way to learn about how to design, run, and analyze studies. In addition, we can offer a list of suggested reading materials that provide you with further knowledge about experimental design and methods.

Bernard, H. R. (2000). *Social research methods: Qualitative and quantitative approaches.* Thousand Oaks, CA: Sage.

This is a relatively large book. It covers a wide range of methods, some in more depth than others. It includes useful instructions for how to perform the methods.

Bethel, C. L., & Murphy, R. M. (2010). Review of human studies methods in HRI and recommendations. *International Journal of Social Robotics, 2,* 347–359.

This article provides practical advice about how to run studies concerning how people use teleoperated robots. In doing so, it provides a resource that would be useful in many similar studies (e.g., HCI).

Boice, R. (2000). *Advice for new faculty members: Nihil nimus.* Needham Heights, MA: Allyn & Bacon.

This book provides guidance on how to teach and research and, importantly, how to manage your time and emotions while doing so. Its advice is based on survey data from successful and unsuccessful new faculty members. Some of the lessons also apply to new research assistants.

Coolican, H. (2006). *Introduction to research methods in psychology* (3rd ed.). London: Hodder Arnold.

This book covers gently all the skills that are required to approach research methods.

Cozby, P. C. (2008). *Methods in behavioral research* (10th ed.). New York: McGraw-Hill.

Cozby concisely explains methodological approaches in psychology. Also, this book provides activities to help you easily understand the research methods.

Leary, M. R. (2011). *Introduction to behavioral research methods* (6th ed.). Boston: Pearson.

This book provides basic information about a broad range of research approaches, including descriptive research, correlational research, experimental research, and quasi-experimental research. It is a comprehensive textbook: You will learn how to proceed through the whole cycle of an experiment, from how to conceptualize your research questions, through how to measure your variables, to how to analyze the data and disseminate them.

Martin, D. W. (2008). *Doing psychology experiments* (7th ed.). Belmont, CA: Thomson Wadsworth.

Martin provides simple "how-to" information about doing experiments in psychology. The author's informal and friendly tone may help start your journey in this area.

Ray, W. J. (2009). *Methods: Toward a science of behavior and experience* (9th ed.). Belmont, CA: Wadsworth/Cengage Learning.

This is a book for the first course in experimental methods in psychology. It is a useful and gentle introduction to how to create and run studies and how to present the results. It does not focus on the practical details like this book does. However, Ray's book can help you learn information about empirically based research and help you understand cryptic presentations in a journal article.

1.5 Questions

Each chapter includes several questions that the reader can use as study aids, to preview and review material. There are also several more complex questions that might be used as homework or as topics for class discussion.

Summary Questions

1. Describe the following terms frequently used in research with human subjects.
   a. Stimulus
   b. Response
   c. Trials
   d. Blocks
   e. Dependent and independent variables
   f. IRB (Institutional Review Board)
   g. Statistical power
   h. Find two more terms and define them.

2. What does "operationalizing the variables" mean in a research study with human subjects?

3. What are the steps in the research process? Create and label a figure showing them.

4. What features make a research study a true experiment?

Thought Questions

1. In research with human subjects, having a pilot study is highly recommended. Why do you think a pilot study is important?

2. We have described some database reference tools in university libraries (e.g., PsycInfo, Web of Science). Choose any topic you like, and then use these tools to narrow down your research interests or questions. Think about how you would operationalize the variables (i.e., independent and dependent variables) in terms of the topic you just chose. If you find previous studies from the database, compare your operationalized variables with the ones in a published study.

3. Based on the overall research process we described in this chapter, write a summary of the procedures you need to follow to investigate your topic in the previous question.

4. It is, in general, important to specify operational definitions of the research variables (i.e., independent variables and dependent variables). However, sometimes it is necessary to gather data to explore a new area of behavior, a so-called fishing expedition. This exploration and data gathering can give researchers new, useful insights. As an example, you may look at the Reder and Ritter (1992) article. In this article, Reder and Ritter designed two experiments testing a range of possible factors influencing feeling of knowing. Discuss what Reder and Ritter observed in the two experiments. Discuss what factors you would explore, how you could manipulate and manage these factors, and how you could measure their effects if you were to run your own study about the feeling of knowing.

5. Within the context of an HCI usability study, discuss what steps in Figure 1.1 you would particularly pay attention to and which ones you might modify or skip.

2

Preparation for Running Experiments

J oining the lab as a new research assistant, you have come to help out and to learn in this area, specifically with running research studies. What do you do? Where do you start? How do you avoid common and easily fixed problems? This chapter describes how to get started. Figure 2.1 illustrates how the preparation process discussed in this chapter fits the overall structure outlined in Figure 1.1.

Consider briefly a usability study evaluating a haptic (touch-based input or output) interface. For this investigation, a lead research scientist or a lead researcher would establish a study hypothesis and design an experiment by first defining what to measure (dependent variables), what factors to manipulate (independent variables), and what environmental conditions to consider. This work would be piloted and would take some time to prepare. Institutional Review Board (IRB) forms would be prepared and submitted. Then, the subjects would be recruited and the study run.

The order of these steps will vary by study, and often they will be done concurrently; thus, the choice of order is somewhat arbitrary. You do not have to follow these steps in the order we present them. The remainder of the chapter discusses each of these steps in this default order.

2.1 Reading Literature in the Area

It is generally useful to have read in the area in which you are running experiments. This reading will provide you further context for your work, including

Figure 2.1. A pictorial summary of the study preparation process, along with the sections (§§) that explain that step.

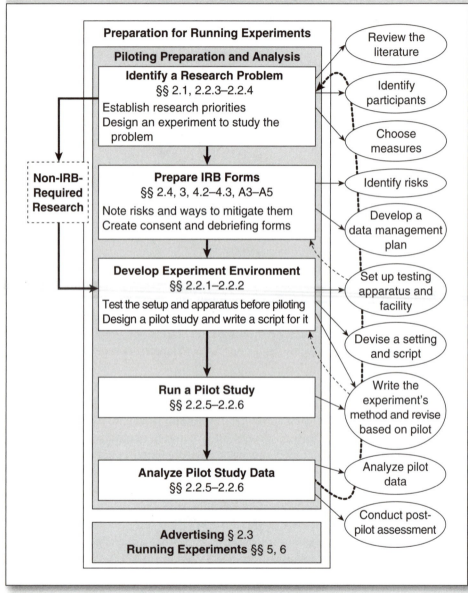

discussions about methods, types of subjects, and pitfalls you may encounter. For example, the authors of one of our favorite studies, an analysis of animal movements, note an important pitfall: that data collection had to be suspended after having been chased by elephants! If there are elephants in your domain, it is useful to know about them. There are, of course, less dramatic problems, such as common mistakes subjects make, correlations in stimuli, self-selection biases in a subject population, power outages, printing problems, or fewer participants than expected. While there are reasons to be blind to the hypothesis being tested by the experiment (i.e., you do not know what treatment or group the subject you are interacting with is in so that you do not implicitly or inadvertently coach the subjects to perform in the expected way), if there are elephants, good experimenters know about them, and prepared research assistants want to know about them!

The reading list for any particular experiment is very individualized. It may be useful to talk to other experimenters, as well as to the lead researcher, about what you should read as preparation for running or helping run a study.

This book does not assume that you have a background in statistics or have studied experimental design. To help run a study, you often do not need to be familiar with these topics (but they do help!). If you need help in these areas, other materials (noted at the end of this chapter) can prepare you to design experiments and analyze experimental data. In addition, most graduate programs with concentrations in human–computer interaction (HCI), cognitive science, or human factors feature coursework that will help you become proficient in these topics.

Many introductory courses in statistics, however, focus primarily on introducing the basics of simple tests, ANOVA, and regression. These tools are unsuitable for many studies analyzing human subject data where the data are qualitative or sequential. Therefore, care must be taken to design an experiment that collects the proper kinds of data. If ANOVA and regression are the only tools at your disposal, we recommend that you find a course focusing on the design of experiments featuring human participants and on the analysis of human data. We also recommend that you gather data that can be used in a regression, because such data can be used to make stronger predictions—not just that a factor will influence a measure but in what direction and by how much.

2.2 Preparing the Apparatus and Materials, Design, and Procedure Through Piloting

A major step in preparation is to prepare the apparatus and materials and find or prepare a place to run the study. As part of this, it is useful to prepare the experimental design and procedure, which interact with these topics. Piloting is an important way to prepare a study.

2.2.1 Care, Control, Use, and Maintenance of Apparatus

What materials and equipment do you need to run experiments? An apparatus is often required to gather behavioral data. In cognitive science, recording user behavior by using experimental software, a video recorder, a voice recorder, or a keystroke/mouse logger are all common practices. There are also tools for generating studies, such as ePrime. Also, some studies require using an eye tracker to gather eye-movement data.

Part of what you will have to do to set up and run a study is to plan the task environment and understand it in detail so that you can prepare it for each session, save the data if the task environment collects data, and shut it down after each session. Experiments in a controlled environment such as a laboratory usually require participants to interact with a computer device, a prototype, or a mock-up. For example, it is possible to implement a task environment in a computer screen—as in an air traffic control task such as Argus (Schoelles & Gray, 2001), a driving simulator such as Distract-R (Salvucci, 2009), experimental tasks with E-Prime (e.g., MacWhinney, St. James, Schunn, Li, & Schneider, 2001), or a spreadsheet task environment (Kim, Koubek, & Ritter, 2007).

As you begin to work on your research task, you are likely to consider several approaches for improving your study. Finding, developing, or modifying the task environment to support your study is often an early consideration. The task environment provides the setting for investigating the questions of interest, and having the right task environment is a key element to a successful study. If designing and implementing a new task environment for your research study seems infeasible, try reusable and sharable environments. With the increasing use of computerized task environments, this is becoming more possible. For example, Argus is available (Schoelles & Gray, 2000), and there are multiple versions of games such as Space Fortress (Mané & Donchin, 1989; Moon, Bothell, & Anderson, 2011) and other games and tasks on the Internet.

After choosing and setting up the task environment, the next step is to determine what method you will use to record the participants' performance. Data collection deserves serious thought. Data can be qualitative (i.e., not in a numerical form) or quantitative (i.e., in a numerical form). Different hypotheses and theories require different types of data to test them and, thus, different methods to collect the data. For example, you can use a camcorder in an interview to gather qualitative information or a keystroke logger such as RUI (Recording User Input; Kukreja, Stevenson, & Ritter, 2006) to measure numerical values of quantitative data in unobtrusive and automatic ways. We suggest avoiding manually recording data—it is hard, takes a significant amount of time, and is prone to error. Sometimes, though, manual data collection is unavoidable, and it is quite often appropriate for pilot studies. Often, with a little forethought, ways can be found to automate the process.

2.2.1.1 Custom Experimental Software

Many studies are performed with custom-built or with proprietary software. The research team conducting the study usually develops these custom applications. They can vary from a simple program to present stimuli and record reaction times to more complex programs (e.g., interactive simulations). If you are a new research assistant, you will be instructed on how to start up and run the software necessary for your work. When you run subjects with such programs, it is useful to think carefully about how the software works and how subjects interact with it. Make suggestions that you think might improve the program's usability as they arise, note mistakes in the program, and observe how subjects interact with the program in novel or interesting ways. These insights can lead to further studies and further hypotheses to test.

2.2.1.2 E-Prime as an Example of a Commercial Tool

E-Prime[1] was the first commercial tool designed to generate psychological experiments on a personal computer (MacWhinney et al., 2001). E-Prime is compatible with Microsoft Windows® XP/Vista. PsyScope[2] is another experiment-generation program, and a predecessor of E-Prime. You can download PsyScope free under a GNU General Public License.[3] PsyScope runs on the Macintosh. You may be asked to use these tools or similar ones in your current study or may find them to be of great value in producing study stimuli more quickly.

2.2.1.3 Keystroke Loggers

It is often useful to record the users' behavior while they perform the task, not just the total task time. This can be done in several ways. Some researchers

---

[1]www.pstnet.com/products/e-prime

[2]psy.ck.sissa.it

[3]www.gnu.org/copyleft/gpl.html

have used video recordings. This provides a stable result that can include multiple details. It also can provide a rich context, particularly if both the subjects and their surroundings are recorded. On the other hand, analyzing video recordings is time-consuming and can be error prone. Analyzing video data often requires examining the video frame by frame to find when the user performs each action, and then recording each action by hand into your data set.

Another approach is to record just the keystrokes or mouse clicks. Commercial versions that will record keystrokes are available from companies such as Noldus (Morgan, Cheng, Pike, & Ritter, in press). We have also designed a keystroke logger, RUI. RUI is a keystroke and mouse-action logger for the Windows and Mac OS X platforms (Kukreja et al., 2006). It is a useful tool for recording user behavior in HCI studies. RUI can be used to measure response times of participants interacting with a computer interface.

Figure 2.2 shows example output from RUI. It includes a header to the file noting who the subject was and the date of the log. There is a header line noting the column contents, with time in elapsed time rather than HH:MM:SS.mmm (the elapsed time seems to work better). You might create similar logs if you instrument your own system.

Figure 2.2. A screenshot of logged data recorded in RUI.

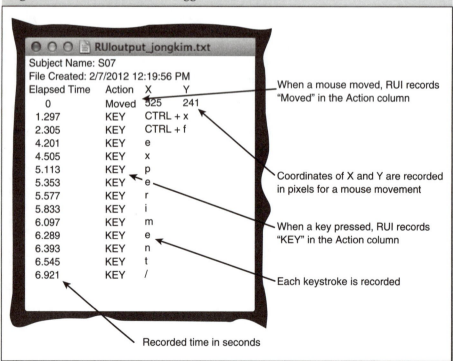

Using RUI or other keystroke loggers, however, can raise issues regarding privacy in public settings such as classrooms. University policies almost universally prohibit installing any tool for experimentation that obtains or could obtain a user's information on identity, such as a login ID or a password (Kim & Ritter, 2007). Fortunately, Kim and Ritter describe one possible portable solution to this problem. They used a simple shell script to run RUI automatically on an external drive, a jump drive. When RUI is operated from an external drive, it provides a way to efficiently use RUI on public cluster machines and then remove it when the study is over. A later version of RUI is also available that anonymizes the keystroke values.

2.2.1.4 Eye Trackers

An eye tracker is a device that records eye positions and movements. Researchers generally analyze the recorded eye movements as a combination

Figure 2.3. Example interfaces RUI can be run on (ER1 robot and the dismal spreadsheet).

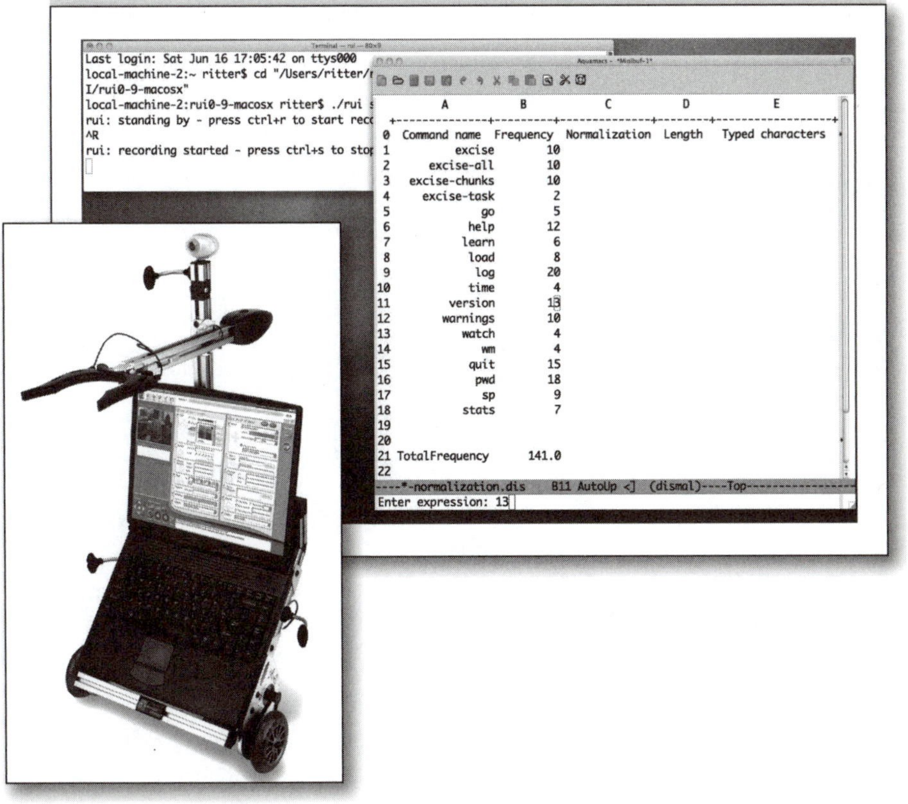

of two behaviors: (a) fixations, pauses over informative regions that are of interest, and (b) saccades, rapid movements between fixations (Salvucci & Goldberg, 2000). Such data can offer useful information about the cognitive processes (e.g., Anderson, Bothell, & Douglass, 2004; Salvucci, 2001) when a user interacts with an interface (e.g., a computer screen or a physical product). This apparatus is sensitive, requiring special care to guarantee the measurement's quality, but over time eye trackers are becoming easier to use and less expensive.

Figure 2.4 shows an individual wearing a head-mounted eye tracker. To the right of the computer display are three monitors showing (from top to bottom) how well the eye is being tracked, what the scene camera is viewing, and the scene camera with the eye's position superimposed. The post on the right with the box on top is used to track a metal plate in the hat and, thus, where the head and eyes are pointed.

2.2.2 The Testing Facility

You will need a place to run your study. A testing facility can be called a psychological testing room, a human factors lab, an ergonomics lab, a usability

Figure 2.4.   Subject wearing a head-mounted eye tracker.

lab, or an HCI lab. Rosson and Carroll (2002) described a usability lab as a specially constructed observation room. In this observation room, an investigator can simulate a task environment and record the behavior of users. The room should be insulated from outside influences, particularly noise. However, it is sometimes necessary to observe and record behaviors of a group of users interacting with each other. In these cases, it may be hard to capture this data in a lab setting. Ideally, the testing facility should be flexible enough to conduct various types of research.

Nielsen (1994) edited a special journal issue about usability laboratories. This special issue provides several representative usability laboratories in computer, telecommunications, and consumer product companies (e.g., IBM, Symantec, SAP, Philips). While this special issue is somewhat dated, the underlying concerns and some of the technological details remain accurate; in addition, many of the social processes and uses for video have only become more important.

If you are designing your own study, you should try to arrange access to a room that allows participants to focus on the experimental task. Lead researchers will often have such rooms or can arrange access to them.

Figure 2.5 shows two different spaces. The space on the left has a room that was built to provide sound isolation by including fiberglass insulation between two sheets of particle board. The doors into the lab, which serves as

Figure 2.5.   Example diagrams of space for running studies. Hollow walls indicate sound-proofed walls, and a triangle on the door indicates a sweep to help block sound.

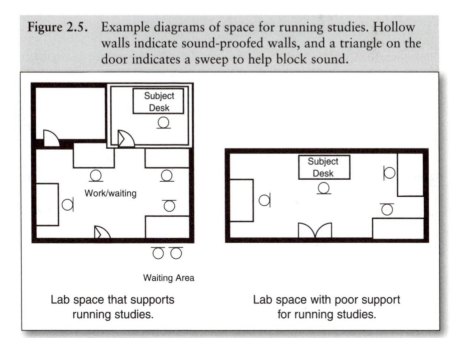

Lab space that supports running studies.

Lab space with poor support for running studies.

a waiting room, and into the running room have sweeps on them to further block noise. The entry room might be a room where students work, but it provides some quiet and a natural place to welcome and debrief the subjects. There are chairs outside the room where subjects can wait if they are early, and (not shown) the room number is clearly displayed on the door.

The diagram on the right side of Figure 2.5 is a poor room for running studies. The subject is in a room where people will be working and, thus, can get distracted while doing the task. There is no place to wait, and because the subject's back is to two doors, whenever someone comes in from the hallway, the subject will be tempted to turn and look, causing noise in the data.

We offer further advice on the setup of your experimental space in Chapter 5, on running an experimental study.

2.2.3 Choice of Dependent Measures: Performance, Time, Actions, Errors, Verbal Protocols, and Other Measures

The point of conducting an experiment is to observe your subjects' behavior under controlled conditions. Prior to beginning your experiment, it is important to consider exactly what you want to observe and how you will measure it so you can effectively summarize your observations and conduct statistical tests. That is, you must choose your dependent variables and decide how to measure them.

2.2.3.1 Types of Dependent Measures

A common kind of observation is simply whether or not the subject succeeds at performing the task. Often, this is a yes-or-no question, and you might summarize your data by calculating the proportion of your subjects who succeed in different conditions (i.e., at different levels of your independent variable). If the task requires repeated responses from each subject, you might calculate the proportion (or percentage) of correct responses for each subject. For example, if the focus of your study is memory, your measure might be the proportion of items correctly recalled or recognized. It is important to think carefully about the measure you use. In the case of memory, for instance, you may find dramatically different results depending on whether you measure recognition or recall. Not only is recognition generally easier than recall, but some independent variables will have different effects depending on which measure of memory you choose. Furthermore, if you choose to measure recall, the type of cue you provide to prompt subjects to recall will make a difference in your results.

Sometimes, determining whether or not subjects succeed at your experimental task requires a judgment call. For example, suppose you are interested in whether subjects successfully recall the gist of instructions presented in each of several interfaces. While it would be simple to calculate the proportion of exact words recalled, that would fail to capture the measure of interest. In such cases, you need to make an informed judgment about the success of recall. In fact, you should have two or more people make such judgments to determine the reliability of the judgments. Your judges should make their decisions "blind"— that is, they should not know which experimental condition a subject was in or the other judge's ratings so that they cannot be unwittingly influenced by their knowledge of the hypothesis or the other judge.

In many cases, experimental tasks are designed so that almost every subject succeeds—that is, responds correctly—on almost every trial. In such cases, the time to respond, often known as *reaction time* or *response time*, can provide a more sensitive measure of performance. For almost all tasks, faster is better, as long as performance is accurate. There are exceptions, of course—for example, the pianist who plays a song the fastest may not be the one who best succeeds at conveying the musical message. When using response-time measures, it is also important to consider the possibility of a *speed–accuracy trade-off*— subjects may achieve faster performance by sacrificing accuracy, or vice versa. Usually, it is easiest to interpret response time if the conditions that lead to faster performance also lead to greater accuracy. And, sometimes, how subjects choose a speed–accuracy trade-off may be of great interest.

Another kind of dependent measure is a self-report. Questionnaires are one common and flexible way to collect self-reports. Questionnaires are familiar from survey research—we have all completed questionnaires in some context— but they can also be used in experimental settings. By answering the questions, participants self-report about the question, thus providing researchers insights into their behavior. The quality and type of these responses, however, depend on the quality and type of the questions asked—so carefully selected and carefully worded questions are important.

One example where questionnaires can be used effectively is in studying self-judgment and its effects. Under certain conditions, our feelings about our knowledge and our actual knowledge may differ. In this case, the researcher may ask the participants to make a judgment about what they know after memorizing vocabulary words. To measure the participants' self-judgment, he or she could use a Likert scale. Likert scales are one common approach and typically consist of five to seven points with ratings ranging from "strongly disagree" to "strongly agree." The researcher would then test the participants and compare the participants' responses about their knowledge with the results.

Another type of data to gather is error data. Error data consist of trials or examples where subjects did not perform the experimental task or some aspects of the task correctly. This type of data can provide useful examples of where cognition breaks down. In addition, it helps describe the limits of performance and cognition. An example of the use of error data to explore mental processes can be found in a study of counting conducted in one of our labs (Carlson & Cassenti, 2004).

Error data is generally more expensive to collect because, in most cases, participants perform the task correctly. Thus, generally, more trials have to be run to gather a hundred errors than to gather a hundred correct responses. Conversely, if errors are not of interest to your research topic, some pilot running of the experiments may be required to generate an experiment where errors do not occur too often.

The measures we have discussed so far all reflect the outcome of behavior—the final result of a psychological process in terms of successful performance, time, or subjective experience. Often, however, research questions are best addressed by *protocols* or *process tracing* measures—measures that provide insight into the step-by-step progression of a psychological process. One example is recording the sequence of actions—moves in a problem-solving process, the timing and location of mouse clicks when using a computer interface, and so on. Computerized task environments make it relatively easy to collect such measures, though aggregating and interpreting them can be challenging. Figure 2.6 shows a trace from an eye tracker of where people finding a fault in a circuit look at the interface.

Sometimes tasks are designed especially to allow the interpretation of action sequences in terms of theoretical questions. For example, Payne and his colleagues (e.g., Payne, Braunstein, & Carroll, 1978) recorded the sequence of

Figure 2.6. Example eye-tracking traces showing different strategies for solving the same problem.

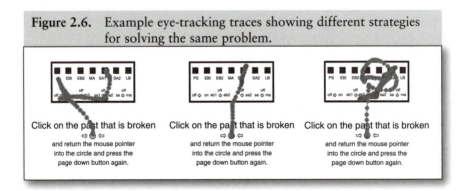

Source: From Friedrich (2008). Used with permission.

information-acquisition actions to generate evidence about decision strategies and processes. Protocols may include multiple streams of data, including verbal utterances, motor actions, environmental responses, or eye movements (Newell & Simon, 1972). The testing methodology developed by Ritter and Larkin (1994) for the principled analysis of user behavior in computer interaction provides an example of the use of verbal protocols. Ritter and Larkin collected talk-aloud protocol data from users of simple interfaces and compared the resulting utterances with a model of behavior of that interface.

Protocol data cannot be reduced to simple averages but can be used in a variety of interesting ways to provide insight into behavioral processes (Sanderson & Fisher, 1994). Often, protocol data are analyzed by comparing them with the predictions generated by computational models intended to simulate the process being studied.

Verbal protocols often provide insights into understanding human behavior. Ericsson and Simon (1993) published a summary of how and when to use verbal reports as data to observe humans' internal cognitive processes. The basic assumption of their verbal protocol theory is that verbalization of human memory (not their view of their thought processes) can be used to derive the sequence of thoughts to complete a task. The basic distinction they make is between *talking aloud*, in which subjects simply say what is in mind as they perform a task, and *thinking aloud*, which involves reflection on mental processes. Talking-aloud data is more valid because it is less likely to be contaminated by the subject's theories of his or her own behavior. Thus, verbalization can be a valid form of data that offers unique insights into cognition. For example, in a learning experiment, subjects can often report the hypotheses they are considering, but reporting *why* they are considering a particular hypothesis is likely to depend on their naïve theories of behavior and is therefore likely to reflect misconceptions about cognition rather than actual cognitive processes. It is also important to consider whether the processes being studied are actually represented verbally—much of our thinking is in a verbal format and, thus, is easy to report, but a task carried out primarily on the basis of visual imagery is much less suitable for verbal protocols. Not only is the need for the subject to translate his or her visual images into words a source of error, but verbalizing such tasks often interferes with performing the task (e.g., Schooler, Ohlsson, & Brooks, 1993). Work with verbal protocols has, for example, helped us understand more about expertise, including how experts play chess (de Groot & Gobet, 1996).

Collecting verbal protocol data requires audio recordings and often comes with special apparatus for recoding and special software and tools for analyzing the results. Collecting, transcribing, and coding such data is time-consuming but can be very helpful for understanding how the task is performed.

It is especially important to have a clear plan for analyzing protocol data and to link the data to the actual behavior observed in the experimental task. In the 1980s and 1990s, the newly respectable use of verbal protocols provided great insight into complex problem-solving tasks. These successes encouraged many researchers to collect verbal protocols, often without sufficient forethought. One of us has several times had the experience of trying—with very limited success—to help a researcher who collected large amounts of verbal protocol data without any plan for analyzing it. In one case, many hours of data collection and transcription were useless because there was no way to link the verbal reports to the actual behavior! (Piloting would have helped uncover and fix this problem early.)

Physiological measures can also provide insight into behavior, though they require substantial investments in equipment and technical skills. Cozby (2004) described several popular physiological measures, such as galvanic skin response, electromyogram, and electroencephalogram (EEG), that help us understand psychological variables. Also, fMRI (functional magnetic resonance imaging) is a popular method of measuring and examining brain activities. If you are interested in learning more about these techniques, see the "Further Readings" section.

2.2.3.2 Choosing Your Variables

Often within a single study, multiple measures with different characteristics are gathered. Some measures are common to HCI or cognitive science experiments. For instance, you can measure the task completion time, or you can measure the number of keystrokes and mouse actions performed by the participants during the task, as well as the time stamp associated with each action. You can also measure what errors were made during the task, and so on.

It is necessary to decide what you are observing and measuring. The decision is important because the choice of measures is directly related to what aspects of the participants' behavior you are trying to capture in the experiment. In general, there are two types of variables: (a) independent variables and (b) dependent variables.

Independent variables cause, or manipulate, the changes in the participants' behavior that the researchers seek to observe during the study. Thus, independent variables are sometimes called manipulated variables, treatment variables, or factors (Keppel & Wickens, 2004).

Suppose we want to measure how humans forget something they have learned. We will return to this example later, but for now, we will focus on the study's independent and dependent variables. Variables that can manipulate forgetting performance include training types, retention intervals (how long a participant will retain learned information), and input modalities (what types of skills a participant is to learn). Thus, we would consider these variables the study's independent variables. They are deliberately varied to create the effects—and they are independent of the subject's behavior. Variables that are fixed going in, such as gender, sex, and age, often are also treated as independent variables because they are not dependent on the treatment. Such variables are sometimes referred to as "quasi-independent" because they cannot be manipulated by the researcher.

Dependent variables indicate what we will observe. Their values are (presumed to be) dependent on the situation set up by the independent variables. Dependent variables can be either directly observed or derived. Often, within a single study, multiple measures with different characteristics can be gathered. For example, in an HCI or cognitive science experiment, you can measure the task-completion time, the number of keystrokes and mouse actions performed by the participants during the task, and the time stamp associated with each action. You can also measure the errors made during the task, and so on.

Response time and error rates are two typical dependent variables. The measures can also be more complex. Workload measures, for example, allow researchers to measure how hard users have to work. The NASA Task Load Index (TLX; Hart & Staveland, 1988; NASA, 1987) directly measures workload using six individual subscales, but sometimes a desired measure is used based on combining them. The choice of dependent variables may influence the choice of statistics used to analyze the data; for example, if there are multiple dependent variables, you may need to use multivariate statistical methods. To sum up, dependent variables are the responses being observed during the study, while independent variables are those factors that researchers manipulate to either cause or change those responses.

2.2.3.3 Scales of Measurement

Variables can be measured using four types of scales: (a) nominal measurements, (b) ordinal measurements, (c) interval measurements, and (d) ratio measurements (Ray, 2003). Knowing these scales of measurement is important because the data interpretation techniques available to you for interpreting the results are a function of the scales of measurement used, and the use of such data—perhaps even how it is stored and the way equipment is calibrated—can depend on what kind of data it is.

Nominal (also referred to as categorical) measurements are used to classify or name variables. There is no numeric measure of values representing names or separate categories. For example, participants can be classified into two groups—a male group and a female group—to measure performance on using a GPS navigation system. In this case, the gender difference is an independent categorical variable to compare performance. Or, if the numbers 1 to 10 are treated as words—such as how often they are said—then there is not necessarily even an order to them; they could be sorted alphabetically.

Ordinal measurements, in contrast, represent some degree of quantitative difference (or relative amount). For example, rankings in a soccer league are an ordinal measurement; they are in order, as are ratings on a scale of 1 to 10. Differences between the first and second team, between 9th and 10th, and between ratings of 4 and 5 and 6 and 7 are not necessarily equal, just ordered.

Interval measurements rely on a scale, with values based on a single underlying quantitative dimension. The distance, therefore, between the consecutive scale values is meaningful. For example, the interval between a temperature of 6 degrees and 12 degrees is the same as the interval between 12 degrees and 18 degrees.

Ratio measurements determine values with respect to an absolute zero—there is no length shorter than 0 inches, for instance. The most common ratio measurement is a counting measure (i.e., the number of hits or misses). For example, in a shooting game, the number of hits is used to determine the shooter's accuracy. Because there can be zero hits, and because the difference between one hit and two hits is the same as the difference between two hits and three hits, it is meaningful to calculate ratios—four hits is twice as many as two hits.

It is important to understand the scales of measurement of your variables for several reasons. First, the scale of measurement determines the mathematical operations you can perform on your data. For example, if you code male subjects as 0 and female subjects as 1, it makes no sense to say that the average gender was 0.3; instead, you would report the actual numbers or proportions. Similarly, while averaging ordinal data seems to make sense, because the intervals may not be equal, an average ranking of 4 is not necessarily twice an average ranking of 2. Second, as a consequence of these limits on mathematical operations, different statistical techniques are required for data on different scales of measurement. Parametric statistics, which include such common tests as correlation and regression, require at least interval measurements. Ordinal or nominal scale data should be analyzed using *non-parametric statistics* such as the chi-square (χ^2) test.

2.2.4 Plan Data Collection With Analysis in Mind

It is quite easy to record data using computer software, audio- and video-recording equipment, or even pencil and paper. Recording data in a way that makes them easy to analyze can be a bit more challenging. You will save a great deal of time and effort, and perhaps avoid the need to repeat the experiment, if you keep these points in mind when planning your data collection.

a. Record everything you will need, including the appropriate identifiers for your data. It is important to capture everything you will want to know about each subject's participation, and doing so requires some thought. For example, you may want to record the time of each key press by the subject; in this case, make sure you know exactly which event begins the timing that is recorded. If you collect some of your data using a computer and some by paper and pencil, make sure you have a foolproof method of matching the computer data file with the appropriate paper-and-pencil data. If your stimuli are randomized, make sure you record which stimulus the subject saw on each trial so it can be matched with the appropriate response. It may seem obvious what should be recorded, but our experience suggests that it is important to think this through carefully. You will never regret recording some aspect of the data—if it turns out to be irrelevant, you don't need to analyze it—but it is impossible to go back and recover observations you didn't make. We know from experience that experiments sometimes have to be repeated because some part of the data that turned out to be critical was not recorded.

b. Organize the data appropriately for analysis. Data analysis software generally expects data to be in a format similar to that of a spreadsheet, in which each line of data in the file represents one case. Make sure that each line of data includes the appropriate identifiers—subject number; level of each independent variable; the specific stimulus displayed, if relevant; and so on. Plan your data file so that each line of data includes the same number of values. If different trials have different numbers of variables—for example, in an experiment on working memory where different trials may require subjects to remember different numbers of items—plan codes to indicate that some variables are not relevant to some trials. One of us recently neglected this and, consequently, had to spend many hours reorganizing the data from a study! Plan data entry carefully, and test pilot data with your analysis software.

c. Choose an appropriate format for data storage. The chances are good that you will find yourself transferring data from one program to another (e.g., from EPrime to SPSS, or from Excel to SPSS). A common format for data storage is comma-separated values (CSV), in which each line of the data file consists of a list of numbers separated by commas. Most spreadsheet and statistical programs can easily read this format. Most programs will also accept similar formats in which spaces, tabs, or sometimes other characters separate values, instead of commas.

d. Plan for data entry. Often, some of your data—perhaps all—will have to be entered by hand. This task, while mundane, is error prone. Make sure that such data are collected in a way that makes it easy to determine how to enter and, if necessary, how to match them up with the appropriate data recorded by the computer. Figuring this out in advance and designing your data file and data collection appropriately can save a great deal of time.

2.2.5 Run Analyses With Pilot Data

We can highly recommend that you run pilot subjects, gather data from them, and analyze the data before launching a large experimental study. The number to run can be found with experience, or by talking with your principal investigator. Analysis of pilot data can provide an approximate baseline of performance or identify problems with the testing techniques or measures used. Your pilot subjects can be your friends, family, or subjects recruited from your subject pool.

An important aspect of analyzing pilot data is that it provides an opportunity to evaluate your data collection plan. You will learn whether your experimental software is recording the data accurately, or whether pencil-and-paper data are being collected in a way that makes data entry easy. One of us supervised a young researcher who failed to analyze his pilot data and learned, after many hours of data collection, that the software he developed was not recording data at all! You will also learn whether the format of your data is appropriate for the analyses you have planned. It is hard to overemphasize the importance of this step in piloting an experiment.

If the results from the pilot data are not what you expected, you can revise the design of the experiment (e.g., change which independent variables are recorded, change the target task, or add other treatments), or the results may suggest an interesting new research question. On the other hand, if the results from the pilot data match your expectations, you can plan to launch your more formal experiments to gather data to confirm the results.

Keep in mind that with a small number of subjects, you might be able to see only large effect sizes. A large effect size means that the difference of your treatment is large with respect to how much people generally vary. For example, freshmen will vary in weight, as will seniors—say, with a standard deviation of 30 pounds. If the seniors on average weigh 30 pounds more than freshmen, the effect of going from freshman year to senior year is about the amount the population varies. In this case, the effect size could be described as 30/30, or 1. This measure of effect size is known as Cohen's *d*. If, however, these students vary in the number of gray hairs on their heads, with a standard deviation of 10, and the seniors on average have 1 more gray hair than do freshmen (an effect size of 0.1), showing that the number of gray hairs differs between these two groups would require measuring many more students than would be necessary to show that weight between groups differs. If you are not finding an effect with a pilot study, you might just need to run more subjects or revise your expected effect size.

2.2.6 Write About Your Experiment Before Running

It might seem odd to bring up writing in a chapter on preparation for running experiments. On the other hand, writing up your study is the final step, isn't it? That seems obvious to many researchers, and that message is conveyed in many textbooks on research methods. However, it is a good idea to consider writing as part of the preparation process—writing about your hypotheses and their rationales, your methods, even your planned analyses. In some contexts—for example, conducting research for a thesis—researchers are forced to do this. The details of your thinking about hypotheses, methods, and planned analyses will never be fresher in your mind than while you are preparing to run your study. Writing can force you to think through possible gaps in your preparation—for example, if you can't describe how you will manipulate your independent variable, you're probably not ready to actually do it. It may not be useful to spend the time to produce the kind of polished writing you will eventually include in a thesis, a technical report, or a manuscript submitted for publication, but it is useful to think about how you will report to others your research question, your experimental method, and your results.

In particular, writing up your method section before you run your study lets you get feedback on the study before it is run. You can show the method to colleagues and to senior researchers and have them debug the study, piloting it in their minds, before you commit further resources to it. It also means that if you write the method before you run and as you run, it will more accurately reflect what you did than if you write it well after the study is completed.

2.3 Preparing for Recruiting

One of the major steps is to prepare for and recruit subjects. This is not always done last but is often easier to prepare than the subject materials.

2.3.1 Choice of a Term: *Participants* or *Subjects*

Disciplines vary as to which term they prefer—*subject* or *participant*—and how the role of the people under study is not completely passive. *Participant* is the newer term and was adopted by many research communities to emphasize the researchers' ethical obligations to those participating in their experiments. Even more descriptive terms such as *learner, student,* or *user* can be applied and are generally preferred. Nevertheless, *subject* is still commonly used and appears in older research. For students in many psychology programs, the term *participant* is preferred by some to *subject.* The sixth edition of the *Publication Manual of the American Psychological Association* (American Psychological Association [APA], 2010) suggests replacing the impersonal term *subjects* with the more descriptive term *participants.* The APA goes on to define *participants* as individuals: college students, children, or respondents. The APA manual suggests doing this but does not require it.

Indeed, the manual (APA, 2010) stops far from requiring the use of *participants.* It says this about the term *subjects*:

> Write about the people in your study in a way that acknowledges their participation but is also consistent with the traditions of the field in which you are working. Thus, although descriptive terms such as *college students, children,* or *respondents* provide precise information about the individuals taking part in a research project, the more general terms *participants* and *subjects* are also in common usage. Indeed, for more than 100 years the term *subjects* has been used within experimental psychology as a general starting point for describing a sample, and its use is appropriate. (p. 73)

Furthermore even within the discipline of psychology, opinion can be split. Roediger (2004), the former president of the Association for Psychological Science, argued against the change to *participants* suggested in the latest version of the APA manual. He argues that *subjects* is both more consistent and clearer, noting that the term has been in use since the 1800s and that it better defines the relationships involved. He argues that the term *participants* fails to adequately capture the distinction between the experimenter and those in the study—strictly speaking, experimenters are participants as well.

No matter how you write with respect to the range of guidance in the APA guidelines, we should recognize that *S, Ss, S's, E, Es,* and *E's* indicate *subject, subjects, subject's, experimenter, experimenters,* and *experimenter's,* respectively, in earlier research. Fitts's 1954 study is one example where these abbreviations are used.

We use these terms interchangeably in this book because we recognize and respect the fact that other research communities may still prefer *subjects* and because not all psychologists, and certainly not everyone running behavioral experiments, are members of the APA.

Another thing to consider[4] in this area is what the purpose of the study is. If the topic of interest to you is a psychological phenomenon—an aspect of human behavior—the people in your study may appear more as subjects in the traditional use of the term. On the other hand, it may be that you are actually interested in how someone performs when given a certain interface or new tool and task. In this case, you are actually interested in how well the widget works. Consequently, your subjects are really more like participants who are participating with you in your work, helping you generalize results and improve the product. In such situations, a term such as *user* may be preferred to *subject*. In any case, take advice about what to call the people you work with.

2.3.2 Recruiting Participants

Recruiting participants for your experiment can be a time-consuming and potentially difficult task, but it is an important aspect. It is, therefore, important to plan carefully for successful recruitment and to take advice from the lead researcher or principle investigator. Ask yourself, "What are the important characteristics that my participants need to have?" Your choices will be under scrutiny, so having a coherent reason for which participants are allowed or disallowed into your study is important.

First, it is necessary to choose a population of interest from which you will recruit participants. For example, if an experimenter wants to measure the learning of foreign language vocabulary, it is necessary to exclude participants who have prior knowledge of that language. On the other hand, if you are studying bilingualism, you will need to recruit people who speak two languages. In addition, it may be necessary to consider age, educational background, gender, and so on to choose the target population correctly.

Second, it is necessary to decide how many participants you will recruit. The number of participants can affect the ability to generalize your final results. The more participants you can recruit, the more reliable your results will be. However, limited resources (e.g., time, money) force an experimenter to find the appropriate and reasonable number of participants. You may need to refer to previous studies to get some idea of the appropriate number of participants.

You can also calculate the power of the sample size for the research study. The power in an experimental study indicates the probability that the test (or experiment) will reject a false null hypothesis. Failure to reject the null hypothesis when the alternative hypothesis is true is referred to as a Type II error. As

---

[4]We thank Karen Feigh for this suggested view.

the power of a study increases, the chances of a Type II error decrease. Most modern statistical books have a discussion on calculating power of the sample size and teach you how to do it (e.g., Howell, 2008).[5]

Finally, you will on occasion have to consider how many subjects are too many. Running large numbers of subjects can waste both time and effort. In addition, the types of statistics typically used may become less useful with larger sample sizes. With large sample sizes, effects that are either trivial or meaningless in a theoretical sense may become significant (reliable) in a statistical sense. This is not a common problem, but if, for example, you arrange to test every student taking introductory psychology at a large university, you might encounter this problem. Section 4.2.1 (Chapter 4) discusses the issue of power further.

Participants can be recruited several ways. The simplest way is to use the experimenters themselves. In simple vision studies, this is often done, because the performance differences between people in these types of tasks are negligible and knowing the hypothesis to be tested does not influence performance. Thus, the results remain generalizable even with a small number of participants.

Subjects can also be recruited using samples of convenience. Samples of convenience consist of people who are easily accessible to the researcher. Many studies use this approach—so many, in fact, that this is not often mentioned. Generally, for these studies, only the sampling size and some salient characteristics that might possibly influence the participants' performance on the task are noted. These factors might include age, major, sex, education level, and factors related to the study, such as nicotine use in a smoking study or the number of math courses in a tutoring study. There are often restrictions on how to recruit appropriately, so it is important to discuss this with those familiar with local policies, such as your IRB or research supervisor.

In studies using samples of convenience, you might distribute an invitation e-mail to a group mailing list (e.g., students in the psychology department or club). This will usually require the approval of the list manager and perhaps others. Also, you can post recruitment flyers on a student bulletin board or place an advertisement in a student newspaper. In a university setting, you may have access to a subject pool—usually students who receive course credit for participating in research studies. For effective recruiting, consider all the resources and channels available to you.

Using a sample of convenience has disadvantages. Perhaps the largest is that the resulting sample is less likely to lead to generalizable results—that

---

[5]Having more subjects gives more power, which allows smaller differences in behavior to be seen.

is, the subjects convenient to you are unlikely to be representative of the general population. Students who are subjects are different from students who are not subjects. To name just one feature, they are more likely to take a psychology class and end up in a subject pool. And the sample itself might contain hidden variability. The subjects you recruit from one method (e.g., through e-mail) and those recruited using another method (e.g., a poster) may be different. We also know that subjects may differ depending on the time of recruitment—those that come early to fulfill a course requirement are more conscientious than those that come late. It is, therefore, important that you randomly assign subjects to conditions in your study, a point we return to in Chapter 4.

The largest and most carefully organized sampling group is a random sample. In this case, researchers randomly sample a given population by carefully applying sampling methodologies meant to ensure statistical validity and equal likelihood of selecting each potential subject. Asking students questions as they go into a football game does not constitute a random sample—some students do not go (thus creating a selection bias for those subjects who like football, who have the necessary time and money, who prefer to watch sports, etc.). Other methods, such as selecting every 10th student based on a telephone number or ID, introduce their own biases. For example, some students do not have a publicly available phone number, and some subpopulations register early to get their ID numbers. Choosing a truly random sample is difficult, and you should think carefully and seek advice about how to do this.

In any case, you need to consider what subjects you will recruit and how you will recruit them, because you will need to fill in these details when you submit your IRB forms (covered later in this chapter).

2.3.3 Subject Pools and Class-Based Participation[6]

One approach for recruiting participants is a *subject pool*. Subject pools are generally groups of undergraduates who are interested in learning about psychology through participation in experiments. Most psychology departments organize and sponsor subject pools. The term *subject* is commonly used in this context, and the APA apparently does not question this.

Subject pools offer a potential source of participants. If a subject pool is available, you should certainly consider it as an option and learn the appropriate procedures and how to fill out the required forms. If the students in

---

[6]Some of the ideas in this section are taken from an e-mail from Katherine Hamilton to the faculty in the College of IST at Penn State (November, 2010).

the study are participating for credit, you need to be particularly careful to record which students participated and what classes they are associated with, because their participation and proof of that participation represent part of their grade.

A whole book could be written about subject pools. Subject pools are arrangements that psychology or other departments provide to assist researchers and students. The department sets up a way for experimenters to recruit subjects for studies. Students taking particular classes are either provided credit toward the class requirement or extra credit. When students do not wish to participate in a study, alternative approaches for obtaining course credit are provided (but are rarely used).

The theory is that participating in a study provides additional knowledge about how studies are run and provides the participant with additional knowledge about a particular study. The researchers, in turn, receive access to a pool of subjects.

Sometimes, researchers can make arrangements with individual instructors to allow research participation for extra credit in a course (drawings and free food do not seem to encourage participation). In such cases, it is important to keep in mind some of the lessons learned by those who have run subject pools. These lessons will be important in receiving IRB approval[7] for this approach to recruiting. First, the amount of extra credit, like financial payments, should not be too large—both to avoid coercion to participate (by offering too great an incentive) and to avoid compromising the grading scheme for the class. Second, an alternative means of earning extra credit must be provided. The alternative assignment should be comparable in time and effort to participating in the study. For example, students might be offered the choice of reading a journal article and writing a two- or three-page summary instead of participating in the study. Usually, the researcher, rather than the instructor, must take responsibility for evaluating the alternative opportunity to keep instruction separate from the participation in research, but this can raise separate issues.

When using a subject pool, it is important to have a research protocol that provides a secure record of research participation and a procedure for sharing that record with instructors to ensure that students will receive credit, while maintaining confidentiality. For example, it is often best to ask for student ID numbers in addition to names on consent forms to avoid difficulties due to illegible handwriting. If you are providing extra-credit opportunities for students in multiple classes in the pool, you should plan for the

---

[7]Further information is available from your IRB. See, for example, www.research.psu.edu/policies/research-protections/irb/irb-guideline-5.

possibility that some students are taking more than one class—you will want to avoid allowing the same person to participate in your study twice. Multiple participation poses problems both of academic ethics (receiving double credit) and internal validity (non-independent observations). It is also appropriate to end the study about 2 weeks before the end of the semester to allow time to enter grades and resolve inconsistencies.

Subject pools usually have written rules and procedures designed to help researchers with these issues. It is important to learn these rules and procedures and to follow them carefully to avoid possible problems.

2.4 Institutional Review Board (IRB)[8]

Investigators in psychology or human factors in many countries now must obtain approval from the appropriate host institution or organization prior to conducting research. The organization charged with approving research applications in a university setting in the United States is called the Institutional Review Board (IRB). The IRB is a committee local to each institution for monitoring, approving, and reviewing biomedical and behavioral research involving humans. The IRB's task is to evaluate the potential risks to subjects (see Chapter 3 for more on potential risks), the compliance of the research with ethical principles and with institutional and government policies, and the suitability of the experimental protocol in protecting subjects and achieving this compliance.

Before the onset of the experiment, investigators must obtain the informed and voluntary consent of the participants selected for the study. The American Psychological Association's Ethical Principles of Psychologists and Code of Conduct[9] specifies that participants have the right to informed consent—that is, participants have the right to understand what will happen in the study (e.g., any known risks of harm, possible benefits, and other details of the experiment). Only after receiving such a briefing can a participant agree to take part in the experiment. Thus, the details of the experiment should be written in clear, jargon-free language, without reference to special technical terms. The participants must be able to easily understand the informed consent form. In addition, the form should enable prospective participants to determine for themselves whether they are willing to participate given their situation and

---

[8]This applies to research in the United States. You should inquire locally, because some countries do not see risk in routine cognitive experimental projects or perform reviews in a more local way or in a way adjusted more to the type of study.

[9]www.apa.org/ethics/code2002.html

personal tolerance for risk. We provide an example of an informed consent form in Appendix 3.

IRB policies are subject to interpretation, so when in doubt contact the IRB representative at your institution. It is useful to think of the IRB staff as coaches, not as police.

In general, IRB reviews fall under two categories, either *expedited* or *full* review. Most behavioral science studies that do not involve the use of experimental drugs, radiation, or medical procedures can be considered for expedited review. Expedited review does not require full IRB committee approval—that is, the full IRB does not have to be convened to discuss your study—and an expedited review can usually be accomplished within a few weeks (again, this will vary by institution and other factors such as time of year). For all other cases, you will need to go through a full review—these are usually scheduled far in advance at specified dates, and this document does not attempt to cover such studies.

2.4.1 What Needs IRB Approval?

Research involving human participants generally requires IRB approval. That sounds simple, but, in fact, it is not always easy to decide when you need IRB approval for activities you consider part of your research. For example, if you or your research assistants participate in your research protocol in the course of developing materials or procedures, IRB approval is not required for your participation for pilot testing, but you cannot publish this data. If, on the other hand, you recruit subjects from a subject pool or the general population for pilot testing or data for publication, you will need IRB approval.

Some other research-like activities that do not require IRB approval include

- administrative surveys or interviews for internal use in an organization that will not be published,
- class projects for which only the students in the class provide data and the results will not be published, and
- research based on publicly available data.

It is easy to confuse these cases with the "exempt" category established by federal regulations. This category of research includes research that is truly anonymous (i.e., there is no way, even in principle, that participants can be identified) and for which the procedures are truly innocuous (cannot cause harm). Examples include the use of standard educational tests in an anonymous fashion, observation of public behavior, or use of publicly available information.

A complete list of research exempt from IRB review in the United States can be found in Title 45, Part 46.101 of the Code of Federal Regulations (www.hhs.gov/ohrp/humansubjects/guidance/45cfr46.html#46.101).

Note that many institutions or funding agencies may require review of research in these categories. For example, Penn State requires that IRB staff, not the researcher, make the determination that research is exempt.

If you have any questions about whether your project is exempt from IRB approval, you should consult with your IRB, or, if you don't have one, a collaborator or colleague at a university may be able to provide information. Many IRBs have special simplified review processes to determine whether particular research projects are exempt from review. It is always better to err on the side of caution and seek IRB approval if in doubt. For example, if you are collecting data in an administrative survey or as part of a class project and *might* want to publish, you should seek IRB approval in advance. The bottom line is that if you are in doubt, you should consult with your local IRB.

Another question arises in research involving collaboration across institutions (e.g., two or more universities, a university and a government agency): Which IRB is responsible for reviewing the research? In general, the answer is that the IRB at the location where data are collected from human participants is responsible. However, this should be established in consultation with your IRB, particularly if you have or are seeking external funding for your research. Some institutions may require that their IRB review the project, regardless of where the data are collected.

If you are working across countries, the U.S. Department of Health and Human Services maintains a compendium of human subjects protections in other countries (www.hhs.gov/ohrp/international/index.html) that may be helpful. Researchers in non-U.S. countries who are unfamiliar with regulations on research with human subjects in their countries may find this a useful starting point.

There are a few other exceptions where IRB approval is not required. If you are running yourself and only yourself or coauthors, you do not need IRB approval. If you are running studies only for class work or for programmatic improvement and not for publication, then IRB approval is not required. These exceptions are useful when you are piloting studies or when you are teaching (or learning) or when you are developing software. Of course, you can in most cases still seek IRB approval or advice for situations such as these. The approval process offers you the opportunity for feedback on how to make your study more safe and efficient. Approval also allows later publication if the results are interesting.

IRB approval is required before any aspect of a study intended for publication is performed, including subject recruitment. Without exception, IRB approval cannot be granted once the study has been conducted. Consequently, you should seek IRB approval early in the process and keep your timeline and participant recruitment flexible. You do not need to seek new approval for finishing early or enrolling fewer participants than requested. You will, however, need to seek approval for finishing late or for enrolling a larger number of participants, or otherwise substantially changing the study.

What if you do not have an IRB? For example, you may be conducting behavioral research at a corporation that does not usually do such research. The first question to ask is whether you really do not have an IRB. In the United States, if the organization receives federal government funding, research with human subjects at that organization is subject to federal regulations. If the organization does not have an "assurance" agreement (an agreement in which the organization offers assurance that it will comply with regulations governing human subjects research) that allows it to operate its own IRB, you should contact the funding agency or the Office for Human Research Protections at the U.S. Department of Health and Human Services (www.hhs.gov/ohrp/index.html) for guidance on having your research reviewed.

If no federal funding is involved, as of this writing, there are no legal requirements in the United States concerning human subjects research. Of course, you as a researcher still have the same ethical obligations to protect your subjects. The next chapter offers further discussion of potential ethical issues. It is wise in such cases to consult with researchers used to working within IRB guidelines for advice; one of us has sometimes done such consultation with researchers in private industry. And, of course, even if your research is not subject to federal regulations concerning human subjects, there are still practical reasons for following the guidelines. For example, journals that publish behavioral research sometimes require that authors certify their research has been conducted in accord with ethical guidelines. Following accepted practices for the treatment of human subjects may also reduce the risk of legal liability.

2.4.2 Preparing an IRB Submission

New researchers—and experienced ones, too—often find the process of submitting their research to the IRB confusing and frustrating. The details of IRB submission will vary depending on the institution and the nature of the research. We include a sample application in Appendix 5. There are, however, a few things to keep in mind that will help make the process smoother.

a. You may first need to be certified to interact with subjects. This means you need to complete human subjects training by reading some material and passing a (typically online) test, showing some basic knowledge about how to run studies and how to treat and protect subjects. Such training is now generally required by IRBs in the United States.

b. Many of the questions you will have to answer will seem irrelevant to your research because they are irrelevant to your research. IRB forms must be written to accommodate the wide range of research that requires review, and they need to include items that allow the IRB members to understand which aspects of the research they must review. For example, this is why you may have to indicate that your study involves no invasive biomedical procedures when it has nothing to do with any biomedical procedures at all. Also, some of the items may be required by institutional policy or federal law. Just take the time to understand what is being asked, and patiently answer the questions. Any other approach will only add to your frustration.

c. Understand that most of the people involved in reviewing your research will not be experts in your area of research. In fact, by regulation, each IRB must contain at least one member of the community who is not associated with the university or organization. This means it is important to avoid jargon and to explain your procedures in common-sense language. Take the time to write clearly and to proofread—it is to your benefit that your submission is easy to read. For example, one of us has a colleague who was frustrated that her IRB did not understand that in psychological terms, *affect* means what is commonly called *emotion*—more careful consideration of using common-sense language would have avoided this frustration.

d. Get the details right. Few of us enjoy filling out forms, but it is especially frustrating to have a form returned to you because some of the details don't match what is expected. One of us had to resubmit an IRB form because of an incorrect e-mail in the personnel list.

e. Allow time. Even with a perfectly smooth IRB process, it may take several weeks for an expedited review. A full review may take longer, in part because full reviews are considered at periodic meetings of the full IRB committee. If you must respond to questions asking for clarification, more time will be required. If there is disagreement about the acceptability of your protocol, it may take even longer to resolve the situation. Plan accordingly.

f. Do what you said you would. While minor changes in your protocol that do not impose greater risks to the subjects generally do not require another IRB review, a modification of your procedure or other changes may require another review. For example, if you decide you want to collect demographic information, add a personality survey, or use a completely different task, consult the IRB staff about how this may affect your approval and how to get a modification approved.

g. Keep good records. IRBs are generally required to conduct occasional laboratory audits on at least a sample of the projects for which they are responsible. If you cannot document your informed consent procedures, show materials consistent with your approved protocol, and so on, the IRB may halt your research while the problems are resolved.

h. Ask for help. Find one or more researchers familiar with your local IRB, and ask their advice about submitting your study. If possible, find examples of approved protocols to use as models for your own submission. And when in doubt, contact the staff of your IRB with your questions.

2.5 Preparing to Run the Low Vision HCI Study

Studies involving special populations are important but challenging because, by definition, they involve groups who have different abilities and often need better interfaces, and studies with them can be more complex. One example paper (Ritter, Kim, Morgan, & Carlson, 2011) starts to take this up, but other populations will have other necessary accommodations. Judy's study (introduced in Chapter 1) was no different in this respect. While Judy's study targets a specific special population—blind and partially sighted individuals—we believe outlining the steps and considerations taken in this study will better prepare you for working with other special populations and, indeed, all study participants.

To conduct her study, Judy and her team had to carefully consider how best to interact with and recruit blind and partially sighted participants; these two considerations are fundamental to studies involving any special populations. The participants in Judy's study differed not only in their visual acuity but also in their opinions regarding blindness and how best to interact with the non-blind world. For instance, experimenters, when describing the motivations for the experiment, had to be careful not to assume that the participants viewed blindness as a disadvantage to be overcome; the schism in the deaf community regarding cochlear implants provided a related warning about this effect. Rather, it was more helpful for experimenters to frame in their own minds visual acuity as a characteristic such as height that entails a set of attributes and considerations. Further, piloting and preliminary consultations with blind and partially sighted individuals proved crucial for developing a workable experimental plan and procedure.

Visually impaired individuals, like other special populations, are a heterogeneous group. Legal blindness is defined as 20/200 visual acuity or less with glasses, or a field of vision less than 20°; however, this general definition masks a whole range of distinctions. Very few visually impaired people have no vision at all or are unable to distinguish light from dark. More generally, partially sighted individuals have blurred vision, restricted vision, or patchy vision. They may have difficulty distinguishing between shapes or colors, or gauging distances. Others may have reduced peripheral vision or, conversely, good peripheral vision and reduced central vision. Judy's experimental plan had to support sighted guiding and room familiarization techniques to help Ss to the experimental room. In this case, participant recruitment preceded the full development of the experimental plan, because achieving a representative sample size depended on the cooperation of outside groups.

Judy's experiment consisted of one *independent variable* (manipulating the navigation bar) and two *treatments* (marking the navigation bar or not marking the navigation bar). The first group (those encountering HTML tags that mark the navigation bar to be skipped unless requested) was the *experimental group*, while the second was the *control group*. The control group used a standard screen reader that allowed the user to skip to the first non-link line; however, they had to request this action. The experiment's *null hypothesis* was that marking the navigation bar to be skipped unless requested *does not help* blind or partially sighted users. The hypothesis's *dependent variables* were the lag times both within and between viewing the web pages. To effectively establish and test the relationship between these variables, Judy took special care when recruiting participants, preparing the experimenters, and ensuring that the apparatus and test facilities met the participants' needs. We will discuss each of these steps, moving from recruitment to lab setup.

Independently achieving Judy's desired sample size ($n = 32$) for two sessions outside of an institution for the blind and partially sighted was likely to be difficult. Working for a midsized company, Judy had to reach out to external groups to find participants. Working with another organization can provide important benefits, such as access to experts and assistive technologies; however, such collaborations can also introduce potential logistical, interpersonal, and ethical challenges. We will discuss the potential ethical implications in Chapter 3. For now, we will discuss some of the logistical and interpersonal challenges.

The challenges confronting an experimenter will largely depend on his or her organizational partner. Institutional partners serving students over the age of 18 are likely not only to be able to find participants but also to have resources helpful to the study, such as access to facilities, transportation, or orientation and mobility (O&M) specialists. On the other hand, these institutions must protect their students' health and well-being and, thus, are likely to demand that the study meet the approval of their own IRB in addition to the IRB at the researcher's institution. Further, you may have to address the concerns of other institutional stakeholders before conducting your study.

If, on the other hand, you turn to an advocacy organization to publicize your study, the degree of institutional support can vary significantly. Support may range from announcements at a local chapter meeting to access to facilities; however, greater support is, again, likely to entail greater institutional oversight, especially if that advocacy organization accepts state or federal funding. When working with an advocacy organization, simply getting the support of its leaders is often insufficient for achieving a representative sample size. Rather, achieving the level of support necessary to conduct a study frequently requires meeting directly with the potential participants and explaining your study's relevance to them. Also, you may need to provide logistical support in the form of transportation and greeters, as well as compensation. Nevertheless, participants recruited in this fashion are likely to take the study seriously.

Judy partnered with an advocacy organization to find participants. Her study required multiple sessions with each subject, which made scheduling harder. Experimenters use multiple sessions for several reasons. The most common reason is to study learning across sessions or to examine the reliability of the measures. In this case, however, it was because the experiment couldn't gather enough data in a single session because it was fatiguing for subjects. In special populations, this last reason may be more common.

Because her study did not examine time-sensitive phenomena such as learning or retention, she was able to meet her goals by scheduling two sessions per participant without regard to interval between sessions. If Judy's study had required her to consider the spacing of her sessions, an institutional partner would most likely have been a better match, because institutions are better able to provide consistent access to participants. Further, Judy's relatively relaxed time demands enabled her to optimize the study schedule to meet the needs of her participants. Judy did have to work with the advocacy organization to provide clear instructions in multiple formats for reaching her research facility. She also had to ensure that greeters were on hand prior to every session to help conduct participants through the building and, in some cases, to meet participants outside of the building.

To greet and work with the study's participants effectively, Judy and her team had to learn both sighted guiding and room-familiarization techniques.

Again, while these techniques are specific to working with partially sighted and blind participants, we include a brief discussion to give some indication of the kind of planning necessary to support studies involving special populations. We do not discuss here related etiquette regarding seeing-eye dogs or participants using mobility tools (see, e.g., Fishman, 2003, and Kim, Emerson, & Curtis, 2009, for more information on these areas). Video tutorials on sighted guiding and room-familiarization techniques are available online, including at www.afb.org/.

Working with a special population will often require appropriate skills and knowledge. In Judy's case, this included sighted guiding, which is a way to escort people who are blind or partially sighted through a new or crowded space (Hill & Ponder, 1976). Sighted guiding always begins with the guide asking the person who is blind or partially sighted—the participant, in this case—whether he or she would like assistance. Simultaneously, the guide should touch the back of the participant's hand with the back of his or her hand to indicate to the participant the guide's relative location (Wisconsin Department of Health Services, 2006). The participant and guide should be positioned along the same direction of travel, with the guide half a step in front of the participant. The participant will then grab the guide's elbow before proceeding, with the guide keeping his or her elbow at roughly a right angle. The guide will then describe briefly the room's configuration, saying, for instance, "We are entering a hallway" or "We are in a large room walking down an aisle, with a door ahead of us." The guide will then indicate every time the pair is approaching a door, a curb, a stairway, or an obstruction (indicating where the obstruction is in relation to the participant's body), or when the pair is about to turn. If the participant and guide need to reverse directions, the pair comes to a complete stop, with the participant releasing his or her grip. The pair then turns toward each other while executing a 180° turn. The guide then reestablishes contact and positioning before continuing.

Finally, we will discuss setting up the experimental space in light of the participants' room-familiarization needs. Ensuring the experimental space is clean and free of distractions is necessary for preparing any study; however, it takes on special importance in this case. Because participants who are partially sighted or blind will rely on tactile and auditory cues to familiarize themselves with the experimental space, the lab setup must feature clear walkways (preferably indicated by a different flooring surface or delimited by a boundary), distinct lab spaces with tables pulled slightly away from the walls (so that the edges are clear through touch), and all obstructions (chairs, trashcans, or hanging objects) cleared not only from any walkways but also from the room's perimeter (Marron & Bailey, 1982). Further, the experimenters should clearly explain all auditory cues, such as tones indicating the session's start and ending, as well as any other routine but unusual noises that might distract the participant. The lab apparatus should feature clear tactile cues, such as buttons that remain depressed while the equipment is in operation. Most assistive technologies already include these features, but a researcher may find it necessary to build experimental equipment to investigate research questions with special populations.

Although Judy's experimenters helped the participants navigate the lab space, it was important for them to be able to get around the lab without the experimenters' direct assistance, including being able to reach the restrooms. Experimental orientation consisted of not only verbal instructions but also moving around the lab space, starting at the perimeter and then proceeding to the center of the room. During this process, the experimenters indicated important landmarks and answered questions the participants had about the room's layout. Next, the experimenters directed the participants to the experimental workspace and apparatus. All experimental surfaces were kept clear of extraneous materials. As the participant moved from the workspace's perimeter inward, the experimenter described each piece of apparatus as the participant encountered it, indicating the key sequences necessary to operate each piece of equipment and answering questions the participant had.

Overall, the preparation steps for this study are the same as for other studies. In every case, you have to consider how to address your participants, how to recruit them, and how to help them arrive safely at your study site.

2.6 Preparing to Run the HRI Study

Human–robot interaction[10] (HRI) studies in general require careful preparation, because working with robots often requires drawing from multiple skill sets (e.g., mechanical engineering and human factors), and the initial configuration of the study components is not simple or easy to hold consistent but is essential for obtaining meaningful results. To be clearer, robots present researchers with a whole host of issues that can makes small changes in the experimental protocol expensive. So it is important to try to anticipate problems early and identify any easy low-cost adjustments if necessary. A few examples can illustrate the issues in this chapter.

---

[10]Also sometimes called human–robot interfaces.

Because of additional expenses in time and resources associated with HRI studies, Bob (the human factors engineer introduced in Chapter 1) should pilot his study. He may find useful results simply from the piloting work. Taking a risk-driven spiral development approach (Boehm & Hansen, 2001; Pew & Mavor, 2007), he will find many ways to reduce risks to the general success of his company's products, and he will find that even setting up the study may suggest changes for the robot design related to setting up the robot repeatedly.

Bob should also prepare his robots and experimental situation carefully. He should try to keep the study sessions otherwise trouble free. Where necessary, there should be backup robots and enough help or time to reset the task situation back to its initial condition. Just how troublesome the robots are and how long it takes to reset the study situation will become clear from piloting.

When Bob reports his results, he will want his reports to be clear and helpful to the audience for whom he is writing. In some cases, this type of audience has a hard heart, in that they do not want to believe that their products are not usable or user-friendly. If Bob confronts this situation, he should consider not reporting his usability metric at all but, rather, just documenting the users' frustration. This is a situation where piloting both study and reporting method may prove essential. If he finds the results on paper are not convincing, Bob should consider including a new measure, such as videos of the subjects. Kennedy (1989) noted that videos of users can be persuasive to designers where plain statistics are not, and Mackay (1995) addressed some potential ethical problems to avoid when using video. Including this measure, however, will require further changes in the protocol, in the apparatus, in recruitment (notifying subjects that they will be videotaped), in the procedure (getting permissions for the various uses of videotape), and in the analysis and presentation.

2.7 Conclusion

This is the longest chapter of this book, in part, because most of the work in running an experiment usually goes into preparing to run it. Some of our advice here may seem obsessive, but we have learned from hard experience that cutting corners in preparing to run an experiment usually results not in saving time but in many extra hours spent repeating experiments or fixing problems. The central point of this chapter is to think carefully about every aspect of the experiment and to make sure you have effectively planned, tested, and practiced as many of the details of the experiment as possible.

2.8 Further Readings

We list some reading materials that may help you plan and run experiments, as well as report the results from the experiment.

Clark, H. H. (1973). The Language-as-Fixed-Effect Fallacy: A critique of language statistics in psychological research. *Journal of Verbal Learning and Verbal Behavior, 12,* 335–359.

This paper reminds us that results for a given task or set of stimuli might not generalize to all tasks or all stimuli. The paper notes that studies with seven verbs and seven nouns might not be able to generalize to all kinds of verbs and all kinds of nouns.

Huck, S. W., & Sandler, H. M. (1979). *Rival hypotheses: Alternative interpretations of data based conclusions.* New York: Harper & Row.

This book provides a set of one-page mysteries about how data can be interpreted and what alternative hypotheses might also explain the study's results. Following each mystery is an explanation about what other plausible rival hypotheses should be considered when interpreting the experiment's results. This book is engaging and teaches critical thinking skills for analyzing experimental data.

Nielsen, J. (Ed.). (1994). Usability laboratories [Special issue]. *Behaviour & Information Technology, 13*(1–2).

This is a special issue of a journal concerning usability laboratories. It reports on several representative usability laboratories—mostly computer, telecommunications, and consumer product companies (e.g., IBM, Symantec, NASA, NCR, British Telecom). It is useful when setting up experimental space, particularly permanent experimental space.

Payne, J. W., Braunstein, M. L., & Carroll, J. S. (1978). Exploring predecisional behavior: An alternative approach to decision research. *Organizational Behavior and Human Performance, 22,* 17–44.

Payne and his colleagues discuss the use of behavioral and verbal protocol approaches to tracing the process of decisions. This article illustrates their use of multiple methods to illuminate the decision process.

Ray, W. J., & Slobounov, S. (2006). Fundamentals of EEG methodology in concussion research. In S. M. Slobounov & W. J. Sebastianelli (Eds.), *Foundations of sport-related brain injuries* (pp. 221–240). New York: Springer.

This book chapter provides you with background for using EEG and its processes, including its physiological basis. In addition, Ray and Slobounov explain EEG research on motor processes in general and brain trauma specifically. It illustrates the spectrum of methods and the level of detail required to perform them.

Rosson, M. B., & Carroll, J. M. (2002). *Usability engineering: Scenario-based development of human-computer interaction*. San Francisco: Morgan Kaufmann.

This book provides comprehensive background knowledge in the area of HCI and gathering data about users in an HCI context.

Schooler, J. W., Ohlsson, S., & Brooks, K. (1993). Thoughts beyond words: When language overshadows insight. *Journal of Experimental Psychology: General*, *122*, 166–183.

Schooler and his colleagues describe a study in which verbalizing while performing an experimental task changed the nature of the task and interfered with performance. They discuss the circumstances under which such effects are likely to occur. Subsequent research by Schooler and his colleagues is also useful for understanding the potential negative effects of verbalization. It illustrates how verbalizing feelings and perceptions can change what the user thinks or remembers.

Stern, R. M., Ray, W. J., & Quigley, K. S. (2001). *Psychophysiological recording* (2nd ed.). New York: Oxford University Press.

This book is useful for anyone who conducts experiments with human participants measuring physiological responses. The book provides not only practical information regarding recording techniques but also the scientific contexts of the techniques.

2.9 Questions

Summary Questions

1. Describe the following frequently used terms.
   a. What is a *subject pool*?
   b. What is *verbal protocol analysis*?
   c. What is required to collect verbal protocol data?
   d. List several types of *independent* and *dependent measures*.

2. What is *error data*? Why is error data expensive to collect?

3. Explain the four types of scales in measurement.

4. What term will you use to refer to the people in your study and why?

5. If you are analyzing photos from a newspaper, do you need IRB approval?

Thought Questions

1. Think about a space to run your study. What changes can and should you make to the space to improve your study?

2. Search previous studies, using the Web of Science or a similar bibliographic tool (e.g., Google Scholar, CiteSeer) and the search keyword *speed–accuracy trade-off*. Choose an article and find out what types of independent and dependent measures (e.g., response time, percent correct) were used in that article.

3. For a study you want to run, consider the file format of the gathered data. Describe the format and generate a sample file. Load it into an analysis tool and perform a simple analysis. Note anything you learned or surprises you encountered.

4. Write the method section for one of the three running example studies (e.g., the partially sighted interface study). The studies are not fully specified, but you can make assumptions. What did you learn from this exercise?

3

Potential Ethical Problems

E thical issues arise when the individuals in a situation have different interests and perspectives. Your interests as a researcher may at times differ from those of your subjects, colleagues, project sponsors, or the broader scientific community, or general public. People are often surprised when ethical concerns arise in the course of scientific research, because they see their own intentions and interests as good. Despite good intentions, however, ethical issues can become ethical problems if they are not considered in the planning and conduct of an experiment. This chapter is concerned with understanding and handling potential ethical concerns.

It is certainly helpful to understand "official" ethical guidelines such as those published by the American Psychological Association (www.apa.org) or those guidelines you will encounter in the ethics training required by your university or organization or your professional organization (e.g., the Human Factors Society, the British Psychological Society). The key to making ethical decisions in conducting research, though, is to consider the perspectives of everyone involved in the research process—your subjects, other members of the research team, other members of the scientific or practice community—and to keep in mind the principles of individual choice, honesty, and minimal risk. This is best done before the study—it is good to fix problems once they occur but better to avoid problems in the first place.

Ethical concerns can arise at several points in the research process, including in recruiting subjects, interacting with subjects during the experiment, handling the data, and reporting the results. As noted in Figure 3.1, we consider each of these stages in turn. All universities and most other

Figure 3.1. Pictorial summary of potential ethical risks, along with the section (§) or sections (§§) that explain each risk.

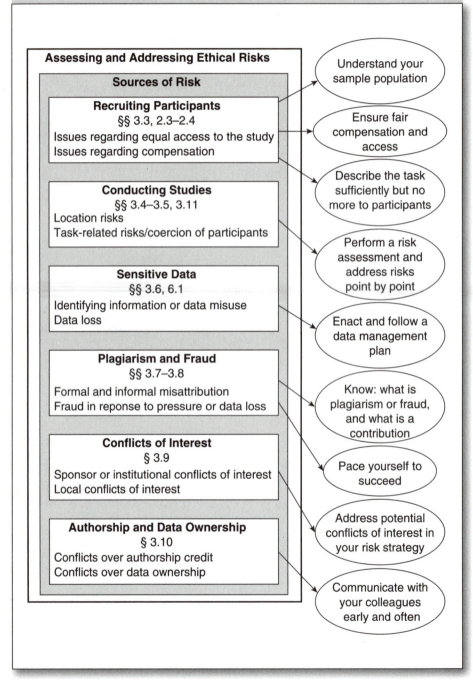

organizations have guidelines for research ethics, resources for ethics training, and contacts to discuss ethical issues. And, of course, ethical concerns should be discussed with the lead researcher or principal investigator (PI).

3.1 Preamble: A Simple Study That Hurt Somebody

One of us was visiting a university for a workshop hosted by a non-behavioral science department. In this story, told in the first person for clarity, the names have been changed to protect all parties. After dinner a "good" student was brought out to present his undergraduate honors thesis work in computer science as part of the banquet. This student—we'll call him Niedermeyer—was studying network effects in his cohort. He was the leader of a large group of students and had made them all participate. I looked at my colleague, well trained in human factors, and said, "Yes?" She said, no, she had no hand in this study.

Niedermeyer then noted that all the students in the study were given Blackberries to record their movements 24 hours a day. This institution is highly regimented, with rules about when and where you can be at certain times of day. I looked at my colleague again, as this movement data could be rather private, and she just rolled her eyes and again said she had nothing to do with the study.

Niedermeyer also surveyed all the participants about their friends in the subgroups, including questions such as, "Would you have this person date your sister?" (It was nearly but not exclusively an all-male group.) My colleague would no longer look at me or accept questions from me!

Niedermeyer then ran an analysis of who in the overall group was friends with whom, creating a social network. In front of the dean, his thesis supervisor, several teachers in the program (not psychology, thankfully), other students at the college, and the invited guests, Niedermeyer noted that his coleader in the group—let's call him Bonantz—did not have any friends according to the survey. To understand the results better, Niedermeyer called Bonantz to his room to discuss this result and to allow Bonantz to explain why he had no friends. He reported to the room Bonantz's response ("Bonantz did not care").

At this point, I had seen just about every aspect of experimental ethics violated by this student and by the people nominally in charge of supervising him, including his advisor and the dean. The student running the study did not take informed consent, he collected and did not protect private data, and he potentially harmed his subject/colleague by reporting non-anonymized data.

As I heard this story, I understood that there was room for experimental ethics education. Maybe I should have stood up and made a piercing comment, but as a visitor, I had little standing, and it would only have hurt Bonantz to emphasize that he had been wronged. So, instead, we use this as a teaching story.

In the rest of this chapter, we review the theory in this area and note some ways to avoid these types of problems.

3.2 The History and Role of Ethics Reviews

We discussed some practical aspects of ethics reviews and working with your Institutional Review Board (IRB) in the previous chapter. Before discussing the ethical concerns you may have to consider in developing your research, it is useful to briefly consider the history of ethics reviews of research with human subjects. Much of currently accepted practice with respect to the ethics of behavioral research arises from concerns with medical and behavioral research in the past century. Many of the regulations governing research with human subjects in the United States grew out of controversial medical research (as can be contrasted with behavioral research). An overview of the history is available from the U.S. Department of Health and Human Services (www.hhs.gov/ohrp/archive/irb/irb_introduction.htm). Beginning in 1966, the National Institutes of Health issued guidelines that established IRBs as a mechanism for reviewing research with human subjects.

The most direct influence on current regulations was the reaction to the Tuskegee Syphilis Study, in which the U.S. Public Health Service monitored the progression of syphilis in hundreds of African American men while failing to offer treatment even after a known cure (penicillin) became available. When this study was revealed in the early 1970s, the U.S. Congress passed legislation creating the National Commission for the Protection of Human Subjects of Biomedical and Behavioral Research. This legislation, the National Research Act, began the process by which IRB review became mandatory for behavioral research with human subjects.

The commission issued a number of reports, the last of which is known as the Belmont Report (www.hhs.gov/ohrp/humansubjects/guidance/belmont.html). This report provided guidelines for research with human subjects, based on the principles of respect for persons, beneficence, and justice. It lays out the basic guidelines for informed consent and assessment of the risks and benefits of participating in research. The report is quite brief and well worth reading to understand the background of the review process conducted by your IRB.

As of 2012, oversight of human subjects research is the responsibility of the Office of Human Subjects Research (ohsr.od.nih.gov/), which is part of the National Institutes of Health. This office oversees the operation of IRBs at universities and colleges.

3.3 Recruiting Subjects

Ethical concerns with respect to your subjects begin with the recruiting process. Obviously, you should be honest in describing your study in your recruiting materials, including accurate statements regarding the time and type of activity required, as well as the compensation provided. Perhaps less obvious, it is important to think about fairness with regard to the opportunity to participate. For example, if you are using a university subject pool, you will have to justify scientifically any criteria that might exclude some students.

Usually, we would like to generalize the results we find to a wide population—indeed, to the whole population. It is useful to recruit a representative population of subjects to accomplish this. Some observers have noted that experimenters do not always recruit from the whole population. In some studies, this is a justifiable approach to ensure reliability (e.g., using a single sex in a hormonal study) or to protect subjects who are at greater risk because of the study (e.g., non-caffeine users in a caffeine study).

Where there are no threats to validity, however, experimenters should take some care to include a representative population. This may mean putting up posters outside of your department and may include paying attention to the study's sex or age balance (correcting imbalances where necessary by recruiting more subjects with these features).

As the research assistant (RA), you can be the first to notice an imbalance, bring it to the attention of the investigator, and thus help address the issue.

3.4 Coercing Subjects

You should not include any procedures in a study that restrict the subjects' freedom of consent regarding participation in the study. Some subjects, including minors, patients, prisoners, and individuals who are cognitively impaired, are more vulnerable to coercion. For example, enticed by the possibility of payment, minors might ask to participate in a study. However, for them to do so without parental consent is unethical, because they are not old enough to give consent—agreements by a minor are not legally binding.

Students are also vulnerable to exploitation. The grade economy presents difficulties, particularly for classes where a lab component is integrated into the curriculum. In these cases, professors must offer not only an experiment relevant to the students' coursework but also alternatives to participating in the experiment.

To address these problems, it is necessary to identify potential conditions that would compromise the participants' freedom of choice. For instance, in the example class with a lab component, the professor needs to provide an alternative way to obtain credit. In addition, this means ensuring that no other form of social coercion has influenced the subjects' choice to engage in the study. Teasing, taunts, jokes, inappropriate comments, or implicit quid-pro-quo arrangements (e.g., a teacher implies that participating in the study pool will help students in a class or between lab mates) are all inappropriate. These interactions can lead to hard feelings (that's why they are ethical problems!) and loss of goodwill toward experiments in general and toward you and your lab in particular.

3.5 Risks, Costs, and Benefits of Participation

Most research participation poses little risk to subjects—a common phrase used in research studies is, "no risks beyond those encountered in everyday life." However, participating in research does carry costs for subjects: They devote time and effort to getting to the experimental location and performing the task. Of course, subjects benefit when they are compensated with money or course credit, or even with the knowledge that they have contributed to research. Nevertheless, ethical guidelines for human subjects require that the researcher weigh the benefits of the research—the value of the data collected, the compensation the subject receives—against whatever costs and risks the subject may encounter. It is common for university subject pools to require that subjects benefit not just by receiving course credit for participating but also by learning something about the research topic and process, usually through a debriefing at the end of the experiment.

Sometimes, studies carry physical or psychological risks beyond those encountered in everyday life. Even very simple procedures such as attaching electrodes for electrophysiological recording come with some risk, as do experimental manipulations such as asking subjects to consume caffeine or sweetened drinks (some people are sensitive to caffeine, and some are diabetic). It is important to consider these risks.

More common than physical risks are psychological risks. The collection of sensitive data, which we discuss next, carries risks, as do experiments featuring deception or procedures such as mood induction. When considering procedures that involve psychological risks, it is important to ask whether these procedures are essential for scientific reasons—deception, for example, often is not—and whether the benefits outweigh the risks. Often, it is important to withhold such information as the nature of your research hypotheses because you want to study your subjects' natural behavior in the experimental task, not their effort to comply (or not comply) with your expectations. This is not deception, because you can withhold this information while truthfully informing subjects about what they will experience in your experiment.

Another example of psychological risk is stress. Stress can result from experimental tasks that place high cognitive demands on subjects, from the conditions in the laboratory (e.g., heat, noise) or from social pressure on the subjects. Sometimes, stress may be manipulated as an independent variable, as in studies of the effect of time pressure or social threat (what someone might think of a subject's performance) on mental processes. It is important to minimize sources of stress that are not relevant to the study and to monitor subjects' reactions to stressors that must be included. In some cases, it may be necessary to halt an experimental session if a subject is becoming too stressed. If stress is included as part of the experimental design, your debriefing should address the need to include it and allow you to address the subjects' reactions.

While it is common to think about risks only in terms of the research procedures, another category of risks should be considered. For example, if you conduct research on a university campus, especially in an urban setting, the time of day at which you hold experimental sessions may pose risks to subjects and experimenters. Participants or experimenters leaving your lab after dark may be at risk simply by walking unaccompanied. This may seem like an everyday risk that has nothing to do with your experiment, but it is something to consider—people have been accosted leaving labs, and it is useful to think about this possibility in planning your study. If you run sessions outside of normal working hours, you should discuss this with the PI.

3.6 Sensitive Data

When preparing to run a study, you should consider how you will handle sensitive data. Sensitive data include information that could violate a subject's privacy, cause embarrassment to a subject, put the subject at risk of legal action, or reveal a physical or psychological risk previously unknown to the subject.

Your research question may require that you collect data you anticipate will be sensitive, or you may collect data that is unexpectedly sensitive. While all data collected from human subjects are generally considered confidential—that is, not to be shared—sensitive data require additional precautions.

The most common kind of sensitive data is personal information. Such information includes an individual's race, creed, gender, gender preference, religion, friendships, income, and so on. Such data may be important to your research question; for example, you may be interested in whether the effects of your independent variable depend on membership in certain demographic categories. Similarly, you may want to collect personal information using questionnaires designed to assess personality, intelligence, or other psychological characteristics. However, when such data can be associated with individuals' names or other identifying information, a risk of violating privacy is created. These data should not be shared with people not working on the project, either formally if you have an IRB that requires notice or informally if you do not have an IRB or your IRB does not have this provision (this may occur more often outside of the United States). You should seek advice from your colleagues about what practices are appropriate in your specific context.

A second type of sensitive data involves subjects' responses that have implications outside of the scope of the study. Some research questions require data about topics such as the use of recreational drugs, tobacco or alcohol use, or medical conditions. For example, if you are administering caffeine and you ask the subject what drugs he or she takes (to avoid known caffeine agonists or antagonists), you may find information about illegal drug use. Or, taking a subject's heart rate or blood pressure measurements may uncover symptoms of underlying disease. Such data can pose or reveal a variety of risks: legal risks if subjects reveal illegal activity, risks to employment status or insurance eligibility, and so on. Data received from other sources may also contain sensitive data. In one recent case, a research sponsor provided database records concerning subjects in a study, and a researcher posted parts of the data on the Internet without realizing that the records included Social Security numbers! Obviously, greater care would have avoided risk to these subjects.

Finally, conducting research can sometimes lead to finding unexpectedly sensitive data. For example, subject comments during a study or before or after a study may reveal that a subject is suicidal.

When an experimenter finds out something that may be dangerous to a subject, the experimenter is ethically obligated to take action, such as referring the subject to appropriate resources. Guidance on these actions is often available from your PI, IRB, or ethics panel. If you don't know what to do, taking contact details and contacting the subject later is acceptable.

These kinds of sensitive data can often be anticipated, and precautions beyond the routine protections of confidentiality can be planned. For example, you may collect and store the data in such a way that they cannot be associated with a subject's identity, instead using identifying codes (subject IDs) to link the various components of a subject's data. Removing identifying information from a data set is sometimes referred to as *anonymizing* the data. However, it is important to be aware that removing identity information may not be sufficient to anonymize data if you have collected demographic information. For example, one study showed that knowing the five-digit ZIP code, gender, and date of birth is sufficient to identify 87% of Americans (Sweeney, 2000). In smaller samples, known basketball players or certified soccer referees in a lab will be uniquely distinguishable. The measures you need to take will depend on the nature of the data you collect and how they will be stored and shared. Your local IRB or ethics review board, as well as experienced researchers, can provide guidance on standard practices.

Under some circumstances, researchers in the United States can protect sensitive data by requesting Certificates of Confidentiality from the National Institutes of Health that "allow the investigator and others who have access to research records to refuse to disclose identifying information in any civil, criminal, administrative, legislative, or other proceeding, whether at the federal, state, or local level" (grants.nih.gov/grants/policy/coc/background.htm). The institutes' website provides more detail on the circumstances and limits on these certificates.

IRBs routinely require that sensitive data—and, in some cases, any data—be stored on secure, password-protected computer systems or in locked cabinets. Extra precautions may include storing the data only on computer systems in the research facility or using the data only in the laboratory, rather than carrying it on a laptop computer or portable storage device. When sensitive data must be shared among members of a research team, perhaps at multiple locations, it is important to arrange secure transport of the data. For example, sensitive data generally should not be transmitted through e-mail attachments.

Data are usually reported in the aggregate, but sometimes you may want to discuss subject-specific responses in writing about your data. For example, in studies using verbal protocols, it is common to quote parts of specific protocols. Skill acquisition studies sometimes display learning curves for individual subjects. Such references to individual subjects should be made anonymous by using codes such as subject numbers rather than potentially identifying information such as first names or initials.

The central point, though, is to be prepared for sensitive data and understand how to address both routine and non-routine situations. If you are in doubt, discuss this with your PI.

3.7 Plagiarism

Plagiarism refers to taking others' work or ideas and presenting them as one's own—that is, without attribution. This includes using ideas from something you have read and not noting that you got the idea from that reading. It includes using direct quotes without attributing the source, and it includes extensive paraphrasing without reworking the concepts or structure, or not attributing the source of the argumentation structure. Particularly in academia, this behavior is taken seriously.[1]

An individual might be tempted to steal others' ideas, research methods, or results from unpublished or published works. Nowadays, manuscripts that are about to be submitted or have already been submitted for review can be available online, making plagiarism easier to perform but also easier to catch.

Why are people tempted to plagiarize others' work? Generally, pressure to meet or surpass institutional standards causes people to plagiarize. To pass a programming class, students might copy another student's code. A faculty member facing review for tenure and stressed by the low number of his or her refereed publications or an RA trying to fill in a review section might be tempted to steal the work of others. Sometimes, the pressure to publish is enough to tempt an academic to plagiarize others' ideas and fabricate their data.

The integrity and development of scientific knowledge is rooted in the proper attribution of credit. The guidelines for giving credit in the sixth edition of the *Publication Manual of the American Psychological Association* (APA, 2010) note that direct quotes require quotation marks and citations, while paraphrasing or in any way borrowing from the work of others requires a citation. You may also need to acknowledge people who give you unpublished ideas for your research. In particular, you may have personal communications (e.g., e-mail, messages from discussion groups on the net, letters, memos) that require acknowledgment. In this case, you will need to remember who gave you the idea (an e-mail thanking them can be a good way to document this) and then cite that person in the text with a date.

3.8 Fraud

We are sometimes shocked by news about research fraud. For example, if a researcher fabricates data and publishes a paper with that data, the

---

[1]If you independently create something and later find that someone else has done similar work, you can cite the other work, and note that it is similar to help readers. See, for example, our Figure 1.1.

researcher is committing fraud. Other scientists trying to replicate the results are often the ones who discover and reveal the initial findings to be fraudulent. While research fraud is unusual, we must nevertheless be aware that fraud can cause significant adverse effects not only for the perpetrator of the fraud but also often for second or third parties such as academic colleagues, institutions, funding agencies, or journal editors. Fraud can also affect more distant people who base key choices on the work in question (e.g., an educational system that prioritizes curriculum strategies based on fraudulent learning data).

If data are lost or accidentally deleted, they are gone; do not replace them without describing how this was done (e.g., running additional subjects). If you did not run a subject, do not run yourself. Such practices undermine your study's validity and are extremely egregious ethical violations. If data are lost, that should be reported. It is sad when you read in an article that "data from 3 subjects were lost," but it is far better to write this phrase than to commit fraud.

3.9 Conflicts of Interest

Conflicts of interest arise when non-scientific interests are in conflict with the goal of doing good, objective research. These non-scientific interests are often financial—a researcher may be aware of what conclusions a research sponsor would like to see from the research. Conflicts of interest can also be local. For example, an RA may know his or her supervisor's favorite hypothesis and which data would support that hypothesis. Conflicts of interest can, of course, lead to outright fraud, as when a researcher fabricates results to please a sponsor. More commonly, conflicts of interest can influence—even unwittingly—the many scientific judgment calls involved in conducting research. For example, deciding that a subject did not follow instructions and thus should be excluded from the data analysis is an important decision. It is important that such decisions do not occur simply because the subject in question did not provide data that fit a favorite hypothesis.

In the long term, quality people at quality institutions working with quality theories grapple with these conflicts in a civil, productive, and routine way. This is how science moves forward. Sometimes the unexpected data lead to drastically new and useful theories; sometimes surprising data lead to questions about how the data were gathered and how well the apparatus was working that day. These discussions of interpretation and measurement are normal, and you should participate in them appropriately and be mindful of the issues.

3.10 Authorship and Data Ownership

Most behavioral research involves extensive work by multiple individuals, and these individuals should receive appropriate credit. "Appropriate credit" often means acknowledgment in published reports of the research. Such acknowledgment may take the form of authorship or thanks expressed in a footnote. Assigning credit can raise ethical issues because the individuals involved may disagree about how much credit each member of the team should receive and how that should be acknowledged. According to the APA's code of ethics (www.apa.org/ethics/code/index.aspx),

> Principal authorship and other publication credits accurately reflect the relative scientific or professional contributions of the individuals involved, regardless of their relative status. Mere possession of an institutional position, such as department chair, does not justify authorship credit. Minor contributions to the research or to the writing for publications are acknowledged appropriately, such as in footnotes or in an introductory statement. (Standard 8.12[b])

While this sounds straightforward, it leaves room for disagreement, partly because each individual is most aware of his or her own contributions. The most useful way to address this is to talk about it, preferably early in the research process. Note that simply performing work in the lab under the direction of someone else does not necessarily constitute a scientific contribution. Useful discussions, but not complete answers, are available (e.g., Darley, Zanna, & Roediger, 2003, pp. 122–124; Digiusto, 1994).

A related issue that sometimes arises is about data ownership. That is, who has the right to decide to share the data or to use it for other purposes? Generally speaking, the PI owns the data, but many other considerations can come into play. In some cases, the data may be proprietary or required to be publicly available due to the sponsorship arrangement.

It is easy for disagreements about data ownership to arise. For example, does a collaborator who disagrees with the PI about the conclusions to be drawn from the data have a right to publish his or her analyses and conclusions separately? Does a student working as part of a research team have the right to use the data collected by that team for other purposes, such as for additional analyses? May a student leaving a lab (such as a graduate student leaving for an academic job) take copies of data collected in the lab? May a student, without consulting with the PI, send the data from a conference presentation to someone with whom he or she discussed the project at a conference? Where the recipient may be at a competing or antagonistic lab? How do the answers to these questions depend on the scientific contribution of the student? Note that data ownership has implications for who may benefit from access to the data (e.g., by publishing the results) and for who is responsible for archiving the data, protecting its confidentiality, and so on. Again, the most useful way to address this issue is to discuss it openly and clearly. Simply relying on future collegiality or unspoken assumptions is likely to and has routinely resulted in problems.

3.11 Interpersonal Conflicts Within a Research Team

Ethics is right conduct. Right conduct interacts with and informs many of the practicalities of running a study, protecting the validity of a study, and also protecting the rights and comfort of subjects. This example examines some of the places where these topics interact.

Research in many academic settings depends on the routine collaboration of more- and less-experienced researchers. These collaborations, while often fruitful and potentially life changing, can present interpersonal and sometimes ethical challenges to both parties. While these challenges can arise from cultural differences, they are often the byproduct of a disparity between the collaborators' research skills and their managerial skills. Cultural differences can intensify the effects of this disparity, but they can also be conflated with them.

While gaining greater technical skills over time frequently entails acquiring more managerial skills, these are two distinct skill sets that require both thought and practice. Consequently, we believe mitigating interpersonal conflicts associated with routine student collaborations requires PIs, lab managers, and collaborating students to address not only cultural-sensitivity issues but also basic communication and project management skills.

Most interpersonal conflicts between collaborating students do not arise from an initial lack of good will but, rather, from an incomplete *theory of mind*—a psychological term that refers to our assumptions about what those around us believe, know, and intend. Until definitively proven otherwise, you should assume that everyone involved in the collaboration really does want to make it work. When we become frustrated or stressed, we can fall back on generalizations to explain apparent gaps in our understanding and that of our colleagues. In some instances, these generalizations can have an element of truth. These generalizations, however, rarely lead to improved understanding or a stronger collaboration. Rather, stronger collaborations arise from a concerted organized effort to establish a common theory of mind. In smaller labs, the coordination necessary between researchers is smaller and easier to maintain, and the researchers know each other relatively well. These informal interactions can lead experimenters to believe that a common theory of mind just emerges, because many of the practices that support it are performed by the PI and, thus, in some senses, are invisible to the rest of the lab. The quality of these processes is often what determines the lab's ability to instill the problem-solving skills necessary for clear experimental insights; alienated students are generally less critical thinkers and observers.

As experimenters begin to design and run their own experiments, they begin to inherit these coordinating duties. Often, lab protocols and procedures make this process easier. On the other hand, protocols and procedures cannot envision every possibility and generally do not operate at such a fine level of granularity as to encompass many of these basic coordinating functions. At the onset of an experiment, a PhD candidate should ask for the basic contact information of any junior RAs assigned to him or her, review expectations, and discuss any limitations. Think broadly, because limitations could encompass unknown disabilities or health issues, scheduling problems, or other situational factors. Simultaneously, be courteous when asking situational questions and limit your questions to what you need to know to help your junior colleagues succeed in the lab.

To better envision the needs of your junior colleagues, ask yourself, "What do I think this student assistant needs to know, and what do I think this student already knows?" Crucially, you need to test your hypotheses by asking junior RAs pertinent questions in a comfortable setting at the beginning of the experimental process, as well as checking with your advisor to verify that you have fully accounted for the information the RAs will need to know to complete their specific experimental tasks. Try to meet with each RA one-on-one if possible. In these meetings, record the RAs' responses. Next, assess each RA's strengths and weaknesses, see if there are any trends, and devise reinforcement strategies that meet the needs of each RA supporting your experiment. These strategies may be collective, such as checklists, or specific, such as assigning personalized readings or conducting individualized training. Group rehearsals are another important way to anticipate the needs of your junior colleagues. Walk through the entire experimental process from setup to teardown with your RAs, and amend written protocols in response to questions or missteps that occur during these rehearsals.

For PhD candidates (and PIs), we also suggest that you check in with the students assisting you in your experiments. You can do this in several ways. First, greet your team members and lab mates—not every interaction with a junior colleague should begin with a problem. Taking a moment or two to greet, thank, or encourage your colleagues can go a long way toward good lab relations. Second, set times to meet with junior colleagues to discuss the experiment and address problems. If a problem has been identified and does not pose a direct risk to anyone involved in the experiment or its success, ask the RA how he or she might remedy it before interjecting your own answer. The student may have an innovative idea, and in either case, you are allowing the RA to take ownership of his or her work process.

If you are working with multiple RAs, make sure you address any problems in performance privately—the point is not to shame the RA into compliance. Also, try to resolve problems at the lowest level possible; this not only encourages a sense of trust but also makes instances where you do need to call in the PI symbolically more significant. In other words, your colleagues will immediately understand that any instance where the PI is asked to intervene is significant and, thus, is to be taken seriously. Finally, distinguish between checking in and micromanaging. Touching base with your team at the beginning of the day, during specific delicate steps, and at the end of the day will allow you to maintain not only situation awareness but also the perception that you value your colleagues' input and time. Otherwise, unless they are making obvious or potentially dangerous mistakes, let your team members do their jobs.

While PhD candidates have obligations to their junior colleagues, incoming RAs, whether graduate or undergraduate students, also have an obligation to communicate and engage. A successful assistantship is not a passive affair. Like you, your senior colleagues are mortals who must operate under imperfect conditions based on incomplete information. From the beginning of your project, try to envision what you, your colleagues, and your supervisors need to know to succeed. Throughout your time in the lab, we suggest periodically returning to this question. Identifying scheduling conflicts or other basic conditions for success does not necessarily entail technical expertise. On the other hand, as you gain technical expertise, keep this in mind. Better anticipating the needs of your colleagues and supervisors, whether in a lab setting or elsewhere, is strongly correlated with success. Also, asking for clarification or reasons for a particular step is important. If framed within the scope of the project, these questions are unlikely to cause offense and will lead to learning. Further, communicating what steps you have taken to resolve a problem, even if imperfect, builds good will and indicates a reassuring seriousness of purpose.

3.12 Potential Ethical Problems in the Low Vision HCI Study

We can examine each of our running examples to see what ethical issues arise. In Judy's study, there are several issues. Studies involving special populations are important because their findings, whether contributing to new technologies or informing public policy, can and have had a lasting effect on the lives of individuals. These effects include the development of assistive technologies, as well as results to support the adoption of beneficial legislation such as the Americans with Disabilities Act. These effects, however, also include products and policies that have led to the profound mistreatment of numerous vulnerable groups.

In light of this history, it is essential that experimenters not only enforce informed consent procedures but also ensure that participants know the experiment is in no way a personal assessment. During Judy's pilot experiments, she found that it was important for the experimenters to explain to the participants that they were not necessarily expected to perform the experimental task to some standard or even to complete it; this diffused tension and encouraged the participants who had difficulty completing the task to explain why, which was a useful result.

As noted in Chapter 2, collaborating with outside groups can introduce both logistical and ethical problems. In Judy's case, her organizational partner was an advocacy organization made up of self-sufficient adult volunteers, some of whom were partially sighted and others not. Judy and her organizational partner did assist with transportation in some instances; however, the participants in all these cases could decline to participate at any time. Participants in the study could choose either to go directly to Judy's office or to meet volunteers at the organization's center, where they would receive a ride to Judy's office. Participants who were unable for any reason to make it to either Judy's office or the center were not contacted again regarding their involvement in the study. In the event that a participant did contact either Judy or the volunteers, a new appointment was scheduled without recrimination. In most instances, we would advise experimenters to avoid rescheduling trials and, instead, to find more participants. In this case, however, Judy's pool of participants was relatively small and there were few instances where this was an issue.

In the one case where a participant was unable to make it to a trial twice in a row, when the participant contacted Judy again, she discussed rescheduling but let the individual know he or she was not obligated to do so. This is a delicate situation, balanced among being sympathetic to difficulties in getting to the study and health problems, supporting subjects who have taken on participation in the study as an obligation they would like to fulfill, and releasing from obligation subjects who cannot make it or whose ability to participate has declined.

Compensation is another source of potential ethical challenges, particularly for special populations. Compensation can be a form of coercion if it masks an essentially mandatory act. With regard to special populations, this most often occurs when the participants' freedom of choice is effectively compromised by their status as members of that group. When working outside of an institution that would provide monitoring, such as a school for the blind, experimenters are most likely to confront this situation when a participant's circumstances force him or her to view participating in a study as more than a meaningful use of time. This was a real concern for Judy because the unemployment rates for persons who are blind are estimated to be between 60% and 70% (American Federation for the Blind, 2012). However, this statistic is not necessarily a direct indicator of quality of life; family support, savings, pensions, and social services are important factors as well. Consequently, when weighing the potential risk of unduly influencing a participant to enroll in your study, a holistic assessment is necessary. Also, it is important to set a fair rate of compensation—generally, 10% to 15% higher than the population of interest's median income rate. This heuristic is only a rule of thumb, but it does generally provide your participants an attractive but not overwhelming option.

Finally, while Judy did not work with an institutional partner, we should briefly discuss recruiting participants from such organizations. As noted earlier, some research questions require routine access to larger subject pools to investigate; institutions are often the de facto choice to find pools of subjects. When looking for an institutional partner that will provide access to participants (as opposed to expert advice or technical assistance), we advise choosing institutions that have an established IRB. While these organizations may insist on working through their review process, the risk of recruiting participants who are coerced into participating is less. Also, these institutions are already familiar with the experimental process and, thus, are more likely to be better equipped to support a behavioral study.

3.13 Potential Ethical Problems in the Multilingual Fonts Study

Edward and Ying's experiment illustrates other potential ethical problems related to interpersonal conflicts. While Ying, the graduate student, had felt that the first meetings with Edward went well, over time she became frustrated with Edward's performance. Specifically, Edward had arrived late to run a pilot subject, had sporadically forgotten to either post or take down the "Running Subjects" sign, and had on two occasions failed to back up data on the lab's external hard drive. With these basic lapses, Ying became increasingly concerned that Edward was making other mistakes. When she brought these issues to his attention, he, at first, seemed to try earnestly to correct his mistakes. Later, however, he just appeared frustrated, saying that he had it under control. Well, Ying wasn't so sure that Edward *did* have it under control, leading her to speak with the PI regarding Edward's performance. While she was busy analyzing the pilot data, Ying knew she had a problem but felt time-pressured herself and thus became increasingly frustrated and angry with Edward.

Edward believed Ying was basically nice but also busy, difficult to understand, and somewhat aloof. Feeling bad about being late and forgetting to back up experimental data, Edward believed a lot of his issues with Ying were the result of poor communication. Nevertheless, he felt awkward asking questions because he did not want to appear to be emphasizing Ying's difficulty with certain English words. Also, Ying's reactions to some of his questions had made him feel stupid on occasion, as if everyone but him was born knowing how to run an experiment. For instance, it wasn't until his weekly meeting with the PI that he really understood why leaving the "Running Subjects" sign up is a big deal or where to check for experiment times. Ying briefed him on the experimental protocol in detail but never mentioned where the weekly schedule was located. In fact, Ying had given him only a day's notice before the study session. He was late to a pilot session only after missing a day in the lab due to an illness. Edward thought Ying would call him and let him know if anything important was coming up. Edward found out about the pilot session only because a friend in the lab had called him.

As for backing up the data, Edward often found himself rushing at the end of the day because the last bus to his apartment complex left shortly after the last experimental session. He hadn't told Ying because he thought it shouldn't be her problem. So, in his rush to catch the bus, he had twice forgotten to back up the data.

To correct these oversights, Edward wrote "backing up data" as an additional step on the experimental protocol that Ying gave him to help himself remember. After writing this last step down, Edward did not fail to back up the data again. Nevertheless, Ying was still clearly concerned about his performance but hesitant to address the issue directly. Instead, she expressed her concern through hyper vigilance. All Ying's double-checking made Edward resentful, which, in turn, made him less focused at work.

Edward and Ying were able to resolve their difficulties. The PI, observing in her weekly meetings a breakdown in communication, pulled Edward and Ying into her office and worked through the initial issues that led to the problems in communication and performance. Sometimes, an arbiter is necessary. This session alone, however, was not sufficient to build a strong collaboration. Edward and Ying, through several weeks and many clarifications, were able to build a routine that worked. This would not have been possible if each had not trusted that, at a very basic level, the other wanted the team and the other person in the team to succeed. As communication improved, performance improved (to a great extent because Edward better understood what Ying was asking him to look for, anticipate, and do), and the team gradually gained more confidence and momentum.

3.14 Conclusion

As this chapter shows, a large number of ethical considerations can be involved in running an experiment. Depending on your role in the research, some of them—for example, authorship and data ownership—may be someone else's responsibility. Nevertheless, everyone who participates in the development and running of an experiment must be aware of the possible ethical problems, knowledgeable about the relevant principles and policies, and sensitive to how subjects are treated, both while in the lab and while the data they provide is being stored, analyzed, and reported.

This chapter notes a few of the most important ethical problems you might face. You may encounter others. If you have questions, you should contact the lead investigator or other senior personnel. In some cases, as in many ethical situations, there may not be a right answer—there may be several right answers. Often, however, there are better answers and good accepted practices.

3.15 Further Readings

American Psychological Association. (2010). *Publication manual of the American Psychological Association* (6th ed.). Washington, DC: Author.

This manual provides useful guidance for reporting your experimental findings in written papers and reports.

American Psychological Association. (2012). *Ethical principles of psychologists and code of conduct: Including 2010 amendments.* Retrieved from www.apa.org/ethics/code/index.aspx

The APA's ethical principles and code of conduct for psychologists was first published in 1992 but has been superseded by newer releases.

Barker, K. (2005). *At the bench: A laboratory navigator.* Cold Spring Harbor, NY: Cold Spring Harbor Laboratory.

This provides an overview of how to run a lab. It is focused more on biology labs, but it has plenty of useful advice for all labs.

Burroughs Wellcome Fund and Howard Hughes Medical Institute. (2006). *Making the right moves: A practical guide to scientific management for postdocs and new faculty* (2nd ed.). Research Triangle Park, NC: Author.

This book provides a theory of the larger context in which research studies are run, including the university, publishing, mentoring, and teaching contexts.

Singer, J. A., & Vinson, N. G. (2002). Ethical issues in empirical studies of software engineering. *IEEE Transactions on Software Engineering, 28,* 1171–1180.

This article provides practical advice about ethical issues in running studies in software engineering. In doing so, it provides a resource that would be useful in many similar studies (e.g., human–computer interaction, systems engineering, and other situations studying work in companies).

3.16 Questions

Summary Questions

1. Describe the following terms:
   a. What are *sensitive data*? Give several examples that you will not typically see in your area, and give several examples that you might see.
   b. What is *plagiarism*?
   c. What is a *conflict of interest (COI)*? What is a *confluence of interest*? Note how many situations will have shared and different interests.
   d. What are some examples of a conflict of interest?

2. How much money would you find to be coercive, that is, that would make you want to participate in a study? How else can you encourage or coerce subjects to participate in a study?

3. Find out about and describe the IRB process at your institution.

Thought Questions

1. Note how the researchers in each running example can anonymize their data. Discuss the way you can anonymize the data in an experiment you want to run.

2. Recall Thought Question 2 in Chapter 1 (the operational definitions of the research variables). Suppose you will conduct a research study with these variables. Discuss how to plan "recruiting subjects" with consideration of ethical concerns (i.e., how to explain your study to subjects, what is the inclusion and exclusion criteria of subjects, how to use a subject pool, how to protect subjects from known risks).

3. For each of the major concerns in this chapter (as noted by sections 3.3–3.11), note a potential concern for each of the running examples.

4. Describe how you would deal with this case: A faculty researcher has gathered data from one research paradigm using public money. A student has been hired to analyze the data using that theoretical framework. After this process, the student starts to analyze the data using a research method that is antagonistic to the original research method and proposes to publish the results showing the first analyses are incorrect. For examples of research methods opposed to each other, see methods in Carroll's (2000) book and Ohlsson's (1992) example analyses resolving how two theories can see the world differently and both be right.

   If you were called in to mediate this case, what factors would influence your decision and what would you suggest to these two researchers?

4

Risks to Validity to Avoid While Running an Experiment

Validity refers to the degree to which experimental results lead to an intended conclusion from the data. A number of things can reduce the validity of an experiment, and these are known as risks to validity. Understanding how subjects will complete the task and working toward uniformity across all iterations of the procedure for each subject are important. The repeatability of the experiment is a necessary condition for scientific validity. There are, however, several well-known effects that can influence the experimental process. These effects are examined in this chapter and are diagramed in Figure 4.1.

Chief among these risks are experimenter effects, or the influence of the experimenter's presence on the participants and how this can vary across experimenters. Besides experimenter effects, there are other risks to the experimental process. We highlight some here and illustrate how to avoid them, either directly or through proper randomization. Understanding other risks to validity, however, will also help you take steps to minimize biases in your data. Even though you cannot eliminate all contingent events, you can note unusual events and, with the principle investigator (PI), either correct them or report them as a potential problem.

Figure 4.1. Pictorial summary of potential risks to validity, along with the section (§) or sections (§§) that explain that risk.

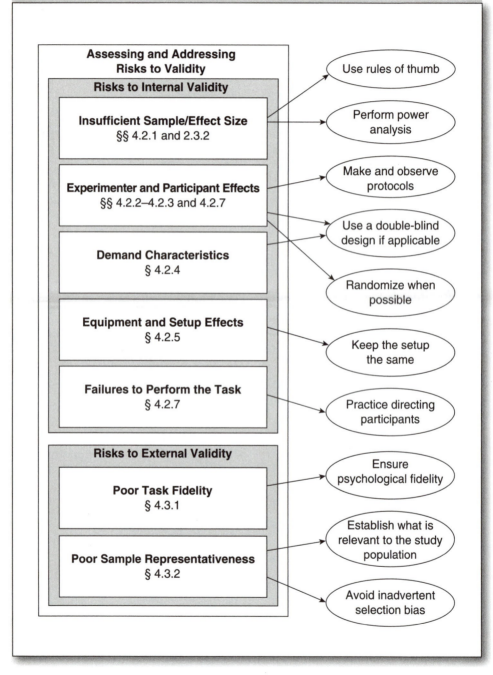

4.1 *Validity* Defined: Internal, External, Construct, and Surface

In general, two types of validity—internal and external—are of greatest interest. *Internal validity* refers to how well the experimental design explains the outcomes from the experiment (or did the effects arise from something else?). The experimental design includes the independent variables you manipulate, the dependent variables you measure, how subjects are assigned to conditions, and so on.

External validity, in contrast, refers to how well the outcomes from the experiment will explain similar phenomena in other situations with other people. This can be viewed as *generalizability*.

Construct and surface validity can also be of interest. *Construct validity* refers to whether you are measuring what you think you are measuring. For example, if you want to measure scholarly impact, counting the number of web pages published does not measure scholarly output as well as number of papers would, which is not as good as number of journal articles, which might not measure the construct of scholarly impact as well as the number of citations. Scholarly impact is, however, a complex construct, so how best to measure it might be multifaceted.

Surface validity refers to whether it looks as though you are measuring what you are attempting to measure. If you are examining how people drive ships, experimental apparatus with boats and ships will appear to have more surface validity than would apparatus with cars. Cars traveling slowly may have the same construct validity, but this may be less apparent to other researchers or readers.

Campbell and Stanley (1963) discussed 12 factors that endanger the internal and external validity of experiments. We need to consider how to reduce or eliminate the effects associated with these factors to obtain valid results.

When you run studies, you may notice factors that can influence the ability of the study results to be explained (this is referred to as *internal validity*). Because you are running the subjects, you have a particular and, in many ways, not repeatable chance to see these factors in action. Good PIs will appreciate your bringing these problems to their attention. You should not panic—some of these issues are inevitable in some study formats. But if they are unanticipated or large, they may be interesting to note or the study may need to be modified to avoid them.

History. Besides the experimental variable, a specific event could occur between the first and second measurements. This may be some current event such as news of a terrorist attack or a disaster that influences subjects in a global way, leading to better or worse results than would occur at other times. Local events, such as a big football game weekend, can also cause such changes.

Maturation. Participants can grow older, become more knowledgeable, or become more tired with the passage of time. Thus, if you measure students at the beginning of the school year and then months later, they may get better scores based on having taken classes in the meantime.

Testing. Taking a test can influence scores on a second test. For instance, if you take an IQ test or a working memory test and then take the same test a second time, you are likely to score better, particularly if you got feedback from the first taking.

Instrumentation. Many measuring instruments must be recalibrated regularly. Some instruments need to be recalibrated such as changes in humidity or head movements for eye trackers. Failure to recalibrate can affect an experiment's results.

Statistical regression. There are risks in selecting groups on the basis of extreme scores. If you select subjects based on high scores, some of those high scores will most likely not reflect the participants' normal performance but, rather, scores that are high partly due to chance. On retests, their performance on average will decrease, not because of the manipulation, but because the second measure is less likely to be extreme again.

Selection biases. Differential selection of participants for treatment groups should be avoided. For example, assigning the first half of subjects to arrive to the first group and the second half to arrive to the second group is unwise. Subjects that come early in the semester to get paid or get course credit are different from the subjects who put it off until the last week of the semester or are recruited in a different way (e.g., posters vs. e-mail). You should do this either randomly or by pairs (split randomly).

Experimental mortality. There may be a differential loss of participants from the comparison groups in a multisession study. Some conditions could be harder or more boring for subjects and, thus, make them less likely to come back in a multisession study.

As you run subjects, you may also see factors that influence the ability to generalize the results of the study to other situations. This ability to generalize results to other situations is external validity.

The reactive or interaction effect of testing. A pretest could affect (increase or decrease) the participants' sensitivity or responsiveness to the experimental variable. Some pretests disclose what the study is designed to investigate. If the pretest asks about time spent studying math and playing math games, you can bet that mathematical reasoning is being studied in the experiment.

The interaction effects of selection biases and the experimental variable. It is necessary to acknowledge that independent variables can interact with subjects selected from a particular population. For example, some factors (such as stress and multitasking) have different effects on memory in older compared with younger subjects. In this case, if you run a group of older or younger subjects, the outcome or findings from the experiment may not be generalized to a larger or different population.

Reactive effects of experimental arrangements. An experimental situation itself can affect the outcome, making it impossible to generalize. That is, the outcome can be a reaction to the specific experimental situation (perhaps the posters on the lab walls) as opposed to the independent variable(s).

Multiple-treatment interference. If multiple treatments were applied to the same participant, the participant's performance could then be invalid because of the accumulated effects from those multiple treatments. For example, if you have learned sample material one way, it is hard to tell if later learning is the result of the second learning method or the first method, or a combination of the two.

Why mention these effects in a book on how to run subjects? Why not just leave them to experimental design texts or courses? We mention them here because if you are a new research assistant (RA), you may not have had an experimental design class. And yet, many of these effects will be most visible to the person running the study. For example, if the RA is running subjects where there is an event, such as an election, and will be comparing the results with those from a different country where the PI is located and where there is not an election in progress, the RA is the one who has the best chance of noticing that something unusual is happening that could pose a threat to the study's validity.

4.2 Risks to Internal Validity

There are several risks to keep in mind, such as participants' effects and experimenter effects, as you set up an experiment and run experimental sessions. We will take these issues up in this section.

4.2.1 Power: How Many Participants?

Human performance can be noisy. Differences that appear could be due to a theoretical manipulation or simply to chance; so you will need to examine multiple subjects to see the range and average of behavior. When piloting, you might start running and not have a fixed number of subjects to run. This might also apply with informal controlled observation for interface and system development. With more formal studies, you will have to get approval (e.g., from your Institutional Review Board in the United States) for a set number of subjects. How do you choose that number?

There are two ways to approach how many participants to run. One way is through comparison to similar research and rules of thumb (heuristics), and the other is through computations of statistical power. Heuristics are often used, and the power calculation assumes that you have an idea of what you are looking for—which you might not, because you are still looking for it!

Each area will have its own heuristics for the number of subjects to run. The number to run is based on the hypothesis and the size of the effect for a given manipulation. In cognitive psychology research such as that conducted by Carlson (e.g., Carlson, Avraamides, Cary, & Strasberg, 2007), 20 subjects per condition is a useful heuristic. In human–robotic studies, the recommended number appears to be between 20 and 40 (Bethel & Murphy, 2010). In (expert) heuristic interface evaluation, the number can be said to be 7 (Nielsen & Molich, 1990), but the range of user types is also important (Avraamides & Ritter, 2002). In physiological psychology, where people do not vary much, the number might be as low as 4 per condition. In areas with more subtle effect sizes, such as education, the numbers need to be larger.

The other way to determine the number of subjects to run is by doing a power calculation based on the effect size you are looking for (Cohen, 1992). The effect size is how much a change in the independent variable leads to a change in the dependent variable. The unit of measure used is the standard deviation in the data. Thus, an effect size of 1 indicates that the mean changes by one standard deviation. A standard deviation is about equivalent to a grade in the traditional U.S. grading scheme. Thus, an effect size of 2 is large (comparable to being tutored individually; Bloom, 1984), and an effect size of 0.1 is relatively small. This is the intention behind statistical tests: to find out whether the changes we see arise from chance or are so extreme that they are unlikely to be due to chance.

We now discuss the power of a statistical test and how a test's power can influence its effectiveness. Calculating the test's power can help maximize the benefits of an experiment by helping you decide how many subjects to run. For instance, while relatively rare, running too many subjects can be wasteful when the effect size is known to be large.

Testing a hypothesis produces two outcomes: One outcome rejects the null hypothesis (H_0) and provides evidence for the alternative (also called the experimental) hypothesis (H_a), while the other outcome fails to reject the null hypothesis—that is, fails to show that the null hypothesis is wrong. When investigators decide to either accept or reject the alternative hypothesis, they can make two types of errors—known as Type I and Type II errors. Table 4.1 describes these types of errors.

In fact, if the null hypothesis (H_0) is true, investigators should fail to reject the null hypothesis. When the null hypothesis is incorrectly rejected, Type I errors occur. The probability of making a Type I error is denoted by alpha (written α). On the other hand, if the alternative hypothesis (H_a) is true, investigators should, in fact, accept the alternative hypothesis. When the alternative hypothesis is incorrectly rejected, Type II errors occur. The probability of making a Type II error is denoted by beta (written β). Experimenters will talk about Type I and Type II errors, so it's worth learning what they are. But we can note that *false alarm* and *miss*, terms taken from signal detection theory, are clearer labels.

The power of a test is defined as the probability of correctly rejecting the null hypothesis (H_0) when the null hypothesis is, in fact, true—denoted by $1 - \beta$. In a practical sense, via the calculation of the power, investigators are able to make a statistically supported argument for significant difference when such a difference truly exists. Good sources for determining the number of subjects to run using power calculations include Cohen's work (listed in the "Further Readings" section), explanations about study size and power in stats books (e.g., Howell, 2008, Ch. 8), and programs that can be accessed online for free, such as G*Power3.

Table 4.1.   Type I and II errors in testing the null (H_0) and experimental (H_a) hypotheses.

Decision Made	True State	
	H_0 Is True	*H_a Is True*
Reject H_0	Type I error (report a result, but there is no effect)	Correct decision
Fail to reject H_0	Correct decision	Type II error (report no result, but there is an effect)

An important point to remember about statistical power is this: Failing to reject the null hypothesis is not the same as proving there is no effect of your independent variable. Knowing the statistical power of your experiment can help you ensure that if there is an effect, you will be able to find it.

Statistical tests such as ANOVA that involve null-hypothesis testing are standard in much behavioral research, but it may be useful to know that a number of researchers advocate more sophisticated approaches. Some researchers argue it is better to report mean results with some indication of the reliability of those means, such as the standard error. In many psychology journals, it has now become standard for editors to require that researchers report *effect sizes*, which are statistics measuring how big the effect of an independent variable is relative to random variation in the data (Wilkinson, 1999). Another approach emphasizes graphic depiction of data with confidence intervals (e.g., Masson & Loftus, 2003). Other researchers argue that analyses should focus not just on the means but on other properties of data distributions. Still others suggest Bayesian analysis, which evaluates the strength of evidence for alternative hypotheses. Some psychologists (e.g., Wagenmakers & Grünwald, 2006) have argued that Bayesian approaches should replace standard significance tests.

In all cases, the recommendations for alternatives to null-hypothesis testing result from concerns about the nature of inference supported by findings of statistical significance. Elaborating on these alternatives is beyond the scope of this book, but it is useful to know that they are becoming increasingly prominent in behavioral research.

4.2.2 Experimenter Effects

When two or more experimenters are running the same experiment, effects or biases from experimenters can exist. One experimenter may unconsciously be more encouraging or another more distracting in some way. Preventing possible experimenter effects is necessary for guaranteeing the validity of the experiment, both for the ability to repeat it and to generalize its results. Mitchell and Jolley (2012) noted some common causes for error that investigators should avoid: (a) the loose-protocol effect, (b) the failure-to-follow-protocol effect, and (c) the researcher-expectancy effect.

First, to avoid the loose-protocol effect, when you run the experiment—and particularly when a study is run by different experimenters—it is necessary to write down the procedures in detail. The protocol document should allow other experimenters to run the experiment in exactly the same way, providing a standardized way to run the trials. Once you finish a draft of the protocol document, you should test it with practice participants. Examples are included in Appendix 2. Producing the final protocol document will require a few iterations of writing and testing the protocols with practice participants and revising the protocol in response to the first pilot sessions.

The second cause of error, the failure-to-follow-protocol effect, results from an experimenter's failure to follow the experiment's protocols. There might be several reasons for not following the protocol, including a lack of motivation to follow the protocol or ignorance of the protocol. Sometimes a failure to follow the protocol can result from efforts to help the subjects. For example, one study found that the subjects behaved unexpectedly in that they had fewer problems than expected. Upon further investigation, it turned out that the student research assistants (RAs) were breaking up the lessons into subparts to facilitate learning (VanLehn, 2007).

The third cause for error, the researcher-expectancy effect, arises from the influence of the experimenter's expectations on his or her interactions with the participants. For instance, I might be biased (consciously or unconsciously) in how I run the experiment if I know I am testing my hypothesis. After all, I have a personal incentive to reject the null hypothesis in this case. Therefore, it is preferable when possible that the experimenters interacting with the subjects be unaware of the hypothesis being tested. When this method is used, it is called a double-blind study—neither the experimenter nor the subject knows what treatment the subject receives. An example of a double-blind study would be when the RA and the subject both do not know which amount of caffeine a subject received or which version of problems was in the subject's packet.

Following consistent, clearly written protocols helps avoid many of these errors. It is also important in most studies to not rush subjects, who are not as familiar with the procedures as you are. Please be patient and give the participants enough time to complete each procedure to the best of their ability.

Depending on the experimental context and the experimenter, experimenter effects can lead to either better or decreased performance or a greater or lesser effect of the independent variables on the dependent variables. The magnitude and type of effect that can be attributed to the influence of the experimenter generally depends on the type and extent of personal interaction between the participant and experimenter, including trade-offs between speed and accuracy. For example, many studies note in their instructions that subjects should "work as quickly and accurately as possible." Thus, you should strive to provide each participant the same comfortable but neutral testing experience.

4.2.3 Participant Effects

Because personal characteristics and histories influence performance, it is important to try to methodically achieve a representative sample of these characteristics and histories when selecting participants, and to assign these factors equally across treatments. Factors such as ethnicity, gender, age, experience, native language, or working memory capacity can all affect performance. Random assignment of subjects to conditions generally helps mitigate the possibility of getting disproportionally adept subjects in one condition. Random assignment, however, can go wrong (or be done incorrectly) or can result in a suboptimal distribution. The RAs who directly interact with subjects often are the earliest, best, and sometimes only way to discover these problems when they are correctable. When you want to generalize to a population, you should be mindful of getting the range of people in a true random selection, which is beyond this text.

4.2.4 Demand Characteristics

Sometimes, internal validity is threatened by subjects' interpretation of the experimental situation. For example, a subject may think that he or she has figured out your hypothesis and deliberately attempts to be a "good subject" and provide the data he or she thinks you want. Conversely, some subjects may try to behave in a way contrary to what they perceive as the hypothesis. For example, one of us, in conducting a study on causal reasoning, was surprised to hear a subject say, "I'm wrecking your hypothesis—I'm behaving exactly the same way whether you look at me or not!" More subtly, subjects may perceive what you think is an innocuous manipulation as an attempt to induce stress, or a set of questions about an interface as an effort to measure personality. Very often, subjects recruited from university subject pools have read about research using deception and assume that all experiments involve some kind of deception.

Even worse, demand characteristics can influence behavior even when the subject is not aware of their influence. The properties of experimental situations that lead subjects to try to behave in certain ways have been labeled *demand characteristics*—that is, characteristics of the situation that seem to demand certain kinds of behavior or the adoption of particular roles. The term was introduced by Martin Orne in the 1960s, and an encyclopedia entry he coauthored provides a brief summary of the concept (Orne & Whitehouse, 2000).

Detailing the wide variety of possible demand characteristics is beyond the scope of this book. However, we can offer some general advice. First, being aware of possible demand characteristics may help you avoid them. It is useful, for example, to ask a few pilot subjects who are naïve to your hypotheses what they thought your experiment was about. Second, clear instructions with as much openness as possible about the purpose of the experiment will help avoid misinterpretations of the task. Sometimes it is even useful to explicitly say that the goal of the experiment is not to assess personal characteristics such as personality or intelligence (assuming, of course, that is true). Third, greeting subjects in a friendly and natural way may help avoid suspicions of deception.

4.2.5 Equipment and Setup Effects

Another common source of variation across trials is the effect of the experimental equipment. For instance, if you are having subjects interact with a computer or other fixed display, you should take at least modest steps to make sure distance from the display is the same for each subject—this does not necessarily mean putting up a tape measure, but, in some cases, it does. It is necessary to be aware that the viewing distance can influence performance and, in extreme cases, can affect vision, irritate eyes, cause headaches, and change the movement of the torso and head (e.g., Rempel, Willms, Anshel, Jaschinski, & Sheedy, 2007). Because viewing distance influences behavior, this factor can be a risk to validity. Furthermore, if subjects are picking up blocks or cards or other objects, the objects should be either always in the same positions or always randomly placed, because some puzzle layouts can make the puzzles much easier to solve (e.g., Jones, Ritter, & Wood, 2000). The experimental setup should not be sometimes one configuration and other times another.

Other variations in apparatus and setup can also pose risks to validity. Avoiding these risks requires careful thought about how subjects' behavior might be affected, familiarity with relevant literature, and careful attention to keeping the apparatus and setup consistent across subjects and experimental conditions (except for planned variations to manipulate independent variables).

4.2.6 Randomization and Counterbalancing

Randomization describes the process of randomly determining both the allocation of the experimental material and the order in which individual trials are to be performed (Montgomery, 2001). *Random assignment* refers to assigning subjects to experimental conditions so that individual differences are not correlated with the independent variables (e.g., sex, order of arrival). The basic idea of randomization is to control for factors that might affect your dependent variables but are neither explicitly controlled by setting the levels of your independent variables nor of direct interest to your research question. Thus, the effect of individual differences, particular stimuli, and order are "averaged out" across the conditions of your experiment, helping maintain internal validity. Of course, the larger your sample of subjects, your sample of experimental materials, or the number of alternative orders, the more effective this averaging-out process is. Statistical methods assume that the observations are independently distributed random variables. Proper randomization of the experiment helps in making sure this assumption is at least approximately correct and allows you to conduct standard statistical tests.

Failing to randomly assign subjects to conditions can cause a number of problems. For example, it might be convenient to run one experimental condition in the morning and another in the afternoon. However, the subjects who sign up to participate in experiments in the morning are likely to be systematically different from those who sign up for afternoon sessions. Similarly, researchers who use university subject pools are familiar with the time-of-semester effect: Subjects who sign up for studies earlier in the semester are often more motivated and conscientious than those who sign up later in the semester.

Random sampling, a related term, is a method for selecting the entire sample group. Ray (2003) noted that one way to achieve external validity is to have the participants in the experiment constitute a representative sample of the entire population. In fact, it is very hard to accomplish true random sampling; however, it is useful to plan recruiting so as to minimize biases that arise when recruiting, as discussed in several sections.

Montgomery (2001) noted that in some situations it is difficult to achieve true randomization because of a fixed variable (e.g., the subject's gender). Sometimes, it may be useful to use what is known as *constrained randomization*. For example, you might randomly assign subjects to experimental conditions with the constraint that an equal proportion of male and female subjects are assigned to each condition. Similarly, if you have two conditions that are manipulated within subjects (i.e., each subject experiences both conditions), rather than randomization, you might assign equal numbers of subjects (randomly, of course) to the two possible orders. This strategy is known as *counterbalancing*.

Practically, there are several ways to randomly assign subjects to conditions. For two conditions, it can be a coin toss; for three or six conditions, a die can be rolled. For more conditions, you can use a random-number generator or a deck of playing cards or some note cards made for the purpose of the study. If you have 30 subjects, roll the die 30 times or shuffle the cards and deal out 30 cards (perhaps from a smaller deck). The order of the cards, dice, or coins gives you the order of assignment. You should check that the balance is correct—that is, that you have equal numbers of each condition. You may also use a table of random numbers (found in many statistical textbooks) or computer software that generates random numbers (most spreadsheets, such as Excel, can do this), or you can randomize an array of numbers in a simple computer program. Random-assignment features may also be included in software packages designed for behavioral research, such as EPrime.

Remember that you are better served by doing balanced assignment—that is, equal assignment to each group. A pure coin flip will not ensure this, because in a series of 10 trials there will not always be 50% heads and 50% tails, and you are better served by doing assignment without replacement. So, creating a set of assignments and then randomly ordering them will work more naturally and efficiently.

Randomization and counterbalancing apply not just to the assignment of subjects but also to the arrangement of stimuli and experimental conditions. For example, if you are conducting a memory study in which subjects learn a list of words or other items, there might be effects of the order in which the material is presented. By presenting the items in a new random order for each subject, any effects of item order will be balanced over subjects. Similarly, when an independent variable is manipulated within subjects, you may want to assign some stimuli to one level of a variable and some to another. Reversing the assignment for half the subjects is an example of counterbalancing.

There are many possible randomization and counterbalancing schemes, and choosing one will depend on the details of your experiment. In general, randomization is effective when there are many opportunities for different random orders or arrangements. When there are only a few such opportunities, counterbalancing is preferred because it guarantees that the factors you are counterbalancing, such as the assignment of stimuli to conditions, are equally distributed over levels of your independent variables (i.e., occur equally often for each level).

4.2.7 Abandoning the Task

During the experiment, subjects' minds may wander from the task. Few subjects will stop using a computer-based task if you are in the room, but a few will stop if you are out of the room (so if this problem occurs with your study, stay in the room!). Some will pay less attention over time, and one way to avoid this is to have shorter experiments. It is also important to strive to run a crisp experiment where your professional bearing and expectations indicate a sense of gravity that will lead them to try to do well.

In experiments using verbal protocols, the subjects may stop talking or talk about other topics. You should neither let them sit without talking nor let them talk about non-task-related things. In the first case, you need to ask them to "keep talking" (Ericsson & Simon, 1993, Appendix). In the second case, if they wander onto other topics instead of reporting their working memory, you may have to ask them to focus on the task. Asking them to do these things is highly appropriate, and if you do not, you will hurt the experiment. You might be more comfortable if you practice this with both a helpful (compliant) and unhelpful (uncompliant) friend as pilot subjects. It is also very appropriate and helpful to put the conditions for such prompts into your script.

Finally, if the subject does wish to abandon the task completely, you need to let the subject do that. In nearly all study protocols, subjects receive full compensation if they start. Withdrawing from a study of the type discussed in this book is rare, but it needs to be accommodated gracefully and graciously. Some subjects who abandon the task will be taking advantage of the situation, and some will have become uncomfortable in some way—and you cannot really tell them apart. In either case, you have to treat them both kindly. Persuading a subject to continue when he or she wants to withdraw may be seen as inappropriate coercion, which raises ethical problems. And if it helps, keep in mind that convincing a reluctant subject to stay may lead to erroneous data.

4.3 Risks to External Validity

It is possible, even common, to run an experiment with excellent internal validity, only to find that your conclusions do not apply in other situations where you think they should. For example, you might conclude from your experiment that Factor X influences Behavior Y . . . and then find that, in fact, the conclusion is inapplicable outside of a lab environment because it applies only to students at your university or from that high school program. This lack of ability to generalize the results is a failure of external validity, or generalizability. Next, we discuss some of the common problems that cause such failures.

4.3.1 Task Fidelity

Most experiments use tasks meant to capture some important aspect of behavior in real-world settings—for example, how feedback affects learning, how display features affect the guidance of visual attention, or how aspects of an interface influence task performance. Usually, though, the experimental task is a simplified version of the real-world situation. Simplifying the task environment is a good and often necessary step from the perspective of internal validity, because it is easier to establish effective experimental control when you use a simplified task. However, if the task fails to capture the critical features of the real-world situation, your results may not apply to that situation. The degree to which it succeeds in doing so is known as *task fidelity*.

Sometimes, the issue of task fidelity is addressed by using an experimental task that is almost indistinguishable from the relevant real-world situation. For example, recent research on driver distraction often uses high-fidelity driving simulators that use actual automobile dashboards and controls, with high-definition displays that update in response to the simulated motion of the car and the actions of the driver. Such simulators allow both excellent experimental control and an opportunity for strong external validity. Other research makes use of virtual-reality setups that allow similar complexity and fidelity. However, such simulators and virtual-reality setups are expensive and impractical for most research, and it is not always clear what features are needed.

What do you do if you can't arrange high-fidelity simulations of real-world environments? The best answer is to make sure you have *psychological fidelity*—that is, that your experimental task accurately captures what is psychologically and behaviorally relevant about the real-world situation. This involves several aspects of the experimental task and its relation to the real-world situation. First, you should consider whether the information available to subjects and the behavior requested of them is *similar* to the real-world situation—do these resemble the real situation in terms of the perceptual, cognitive, and motor aspects of the behavior? Second, you should consider whether the experimental situation is *representative* of the real situation—for example, do the cues available predict other cues or outcomes in the same way (with the same probability or subject to the same contextual influences) as in the real situation? This may require careful thinking about the frequency with which subjects encounter particular stimuli, for example. Psychological fidelity thus involves both resemblance and structure (for further discussion, see Dhami & Hertwig, 2004; Kirlik, 2010; Smallman & St. John, 2005). It may be easiest to understand the issue of psychological fidelity by considering some examples in which generalization has or has not been successful.

Early in the history of research on memory, Ebbinghaus (1885/1964) decided he could best achieve experimental control by using nonsense syllables (syllables such as GAX that have no meaning) to avoid the influence of prior learning. However, in real-world memory situations, people rely on associations to prior knowledge as a basis for remembering. Thus, many of Ebbinghaus's results, while they can be repeated, are difficult to generalize to the real world. For example, he provided an elegant description of the relation between repetition and memory, but in the real world, some things are memorable after a single repetition because they are not nonsense sylla-bles, while others are much harder to learn because they are.

Studies of learning and training provide many examples of both success-ful and unsuccessful generalization. In these studies, the research question often focuses on whether learning in a simplified or simulated training envi-ronment can be transferred to a real task environment and whether the variables that affect learning in the training environment predict perfor-mance in the real task environment. For example, Cassavaugh and Kramer (2009) reported that the effects of training in relatively simple tasks general-ized to driving by older adults in a high-fidelity driving simulator. On the other hand, Lintern, Sheppard, Parker, Yates, and Nolan (1989) found in a study of simulator training for military flight that the simulators that pro-duced the best performance in training were not the ones that resulted in the best performance in actual flights. These results suggest that careful analysis of the perceptual and cognitive components of the task (of driving and fly-ing) need to capture the relevant similarities to be generalizable, rather than simply the surface features (Smallman & St. John, 2005).

Evaluating the external validity of your experimental task is not a simple question and must be answered not by a subjective judgment of how similar your task is to the real-world situation of interest but, rather, by a systematic consideration of what aspects of the task are important. Proctor and Dutta (1995, Ch. 9) provided a useful introduction to this issue in the context of training research.

4.3.2 Representativeness of Your Sample

We mentioned earlier the value of recruiting a broad sample of subjects. The field of psychology has often been criticized for conducting research primarily with college students in Western cultures. While the argument can be made that restricting research to this kind of sample is fine for studying very basic processes not expected to differ from person to person, that argu-ment breaks down when we consider many research questions relevant to real life. For example, older individuals often employ different strategies for prospective memory (remembering to do things) than do college-age sub-jects. Icons and instructions that are easy for American college students to interpret may be completely opaque to people living in other cultures.

So, try to select a broad representative sample of subjects if you want gen-eralizability. When you prepare posters or other advertising materials, we encourage you to be general about the contents of the study. If you are specific about your study ("Math puzzle fun doing repeated serial subtraction"), you will probably reach only a subset of what is likely your target population. In the "math fun" case, people who really like to do math will sign up, and you will not draw a cross-section of your population. If you instead say simply that the study is about "routine mental processes," you will encourage less self-selection by potential subjects. Also, if you create a "fun" poster, this can lead to an escalation across research groups, all trying to present more "fun" experiments with their posters and unrealistically raising subjects' expectations.

Listing all the ways a restricted sample of subjects can make it hard to generalize experimental results could fill a book (e.g., Jonassen & Grabowski, 1993). The important point is that you should think about the situations to which you want to generalize and ask yourself how your sample might differ from the population in the desired situation. The best thing, of course, is to recruit subjects who are representative of the population of interest.

4.4 Avoiding Risks in the Multilingual Fonts Study

The running examples contain several lessons about reducing risk. If we examine Ying and Edward's study, we find that threats to internal validity can emerge both from serious contextual issues that require explicit steps be taken during the design, approval, and recruitment stages of the experiment, and from avoiding seemingly innocuous oversights that nevertheless can jeopardize the experiment's internal validity. Counteracting these threats requires vigilance, cooperation, and sometimes creativity from the whole team. We will discuss both sets of problems within the context of this study here and in Chapter 5.

As noted previously, internal validity refers to whether we can assert with any confidence that changes in the independent variable reliably lead to changes in the dependent variable or variables. To establish internal validity, we must show, at a minimum, that cause precedes effect (temporal precedence), that cause and effect are related (covariance), and that no plausible alternative hypothesis exists that better explains the correlation found between the variables (nonspuriousness). Threats to internal validity are any factor or combination of factors that introduce ambiguity as to the nature of the relationship being studied. These threats can include but are not limited to confounding variables, selection bias, historical or situational factors, maturation, repeated testing, and experimenter biases.

At the onset, Ying and Edward faced a serious problem: achieving a large enough representative sample size. After completing a power analysis (Cohen, 1988, 1992), Ying found that she needed at least 30 participants per alphabet she was using (Arabic and Hangul)—a minimum of 60 participants. Previous studies examining matrix formats for non-Roman alphabets have primarily occurred outside of the United States. Finding participants with fluency in the alphabet of interest posed a significant challenge. This challenge was further complicated by the external validity concerns of key stakeholders within the inexpensive laptop project—whether the results would be generalizable outside of the experimental setting. To satisfy these stakeholders, a condition for the study was to test all participants using interfaces featuring the screen resolution and size found on inexpensive laptops to ensure the matrix formats would be evaluated under conditions similar to those of the children in the program. While keeping the screen size and resolution constant across experimental conditions was necessary for internal validity, usually human–computer interaction studies feature larger (desktop) screens with better resolution. In either case, the need to control for both factors made an online study impractical.

Using flyers and the departmental newsletter enabled Ying and Edward to find enough participants for a pilot study: 15. These methods alone, however, were insufficient to get the 60 participants necessary for the study. Ultimately, Ying and Edward had to contact student groups associated with these populations. Consequently, while the participants all had sufficient fluency in English to complete the study, some participants—generally friends and family of graduate students—required additional instructions and handouts in their own languages, as well as maps to the lab. In addition, scheduling participants required flexibility and a willingness to accommodate parental obligations of young parents. But, by planning and getting more resources (including time) than had originally been budgeted, the study could be completed.

4.5 Avoiding Risks in the HRI Study

In preparing his study and recruiting subjects, Bob particularly needs to worry about risks to external validity: Do the results impact his users, his robots, and the tasks and situation in which they will frequently be used? Bob's company will be interested in the generalizability of his results and not simply whether the results speak to the particular situation he was able to study. So he should take care that the subjects he uses are similar to the robot's potential users. If the robot is for the elderly or for children, he should have elderly or children users. He should not have the engineers who already know how to use the robot, because they helped build it (even though some of them will think they are like the target users or that they can "pretend" to be like them). Thinking you are like users if you are the designer is a fundamental attribution error for design (Ritter, Baxter, & Churchill, in press, Ch. 1). Bob should also be cautious about including friends, neighbors, or colleagues of the engineers among his participants. These people may have spoken with the engineers or worked with them and might know too much to represent the user population accurately, or may only want to report good things about the robots.

Bob should also take some care that the tasks and the environment are operationally similar to the tasks required of the robot and its operators in their intended environment. If the robots are for engineers in research and development firms, then he is set, because the robots are already in their natural setting. If, on the other hand, the robots are for disaster relief workers, he will need a situation similar to those the robot will have to face and users similar to its intended operators—for example, a pile of rubble and a fireman (not undergraduate or graduate students)—to help test the robots (see, e.g., Murphy, Blitch, & Casper, 2002).

4.6 Conclusion

We have discussed here some of the major threats to internal and external validity. There are too many possible threats to address them all, but being aware of the types of threats can help you design and run a better experiment. Perhaps more important, thinking about the threats discussed here can help make you aware of possible limitations of your experiment and let you recognize other threats to validity we have not discussed.

4.7 Further Readings

Cohen, J. (1992). A power primer. *Psychological Bulletin, 112,* 155–159.
Cohen, J. (1992). Statistical power analysis. *Current Directions in Psychological Science, 1,* 98–101.

> Cohen has been raising the issue of the importance of statistical power analysis since the 1960s. He originated the statistical measure of power—that is, of measuring the effect of a manipulation in terms of the natural variation in the measurements and effect sizes. These two articles above will help you be aware of this issue and avoid Type I (false alarms) and II errors (misses) in your research experiments.

Ericsson, K. A., & Simon, H. A. (1993). *Protocol analysis: Verbal reports as data* (2nd ed.). Cambridge: MIT Press.

> Ericsson and Simon explain the theory of how verbal protocols can be used, in what ways they are valid, and when they are invalid. Their journal article (Ericsson & Simon, 1980) is shorter but now less up to date.

Howell, D. C. (2007). *Statistical methods for psychology* (6th ed.). Belmont, CA: Thomson.

> Howell's book provides a useful summary of how to compute power. It is written for those learning statistics. Other introductory statistics books will have similar treatments. They are useful introductions to this process.

4.8 Questions

Summary Questions

1. Describe the following terms:
   a. What is the *experimenter effect*?
   b. What is *randomization* (random assignment)?
   c. What is *random selection*?
   d. What is *fraud*?
   e. What is *generalizability*?
   f. What is *effect size*?
   g. What is *selection bias*?

2. Describe your research project, and then list 12 factors that can endanger the validity of your research with human subjects (i.e., internal and external validity issues).

3. Explain Type I and Type II errors in testing a research hypothesis.

4. If you have a choice, are you willing to sacrifice internal validity for external validity?

Thought Questions

1. Recall Thought Question 2 in Chapter 1 (the operational definitions of the research variables). Suppose that you will conduct a research study with these variables. Discuss whether there are risks that might endanger the validity of your research. Discuss how you plan to mitigate the risks.

2. If you run a study using university freshmen, explain what this will mean for your results. If you run a study using people recruited from a newspaper ad, explain what this will mean for your results.

3. Within your own study, what do you think are the biggest risks to the results being true (internal validity) and generalizable (external validity)?

4. If your study's results cannot be generalized to any other situation, should it be run? Discuss.

5

Running a Research Session

This chapter provides practical information on what to do when you run a research session. We assume that you have developed your initial experimental design and are now ready to run a pilot study. This chapter is thus about interacting with subjects and the context in which you do that.

There are two main sections, preparing for a session and running the session. Accompanying figures summarize the steps. This chapter also notes other issues that can arise while running a study, including computer simulations (models) as subjects, missing subjects, and other problems.

5.1 Preparing to Run a Research Session

There are several steps for preparing a study. Some of these steps are done much earlier, such as piloting the study to prepare in general, and some are done on the day of a session to prepare for the next subject. Figure 5.1 provides a graphical overview of the process of preparing a study.

5.1.1 Preparing the Space for Your Study

The environment you provide for your subjects directly influences the quality of your data. Typically, preparing the space for your experiment will seem straightforward—often, subjects will simply sit at a computer and perform the experimental task. However, giving some thought to setting up the space in advance can help. For example, if possible, you should provide an adjustable-height chair if subjects are sitting at a computer. Minimizing

Figure 5.1. A pictorial summary of preparing a research session, along with the section (§) or sections (§§) that explain each step.

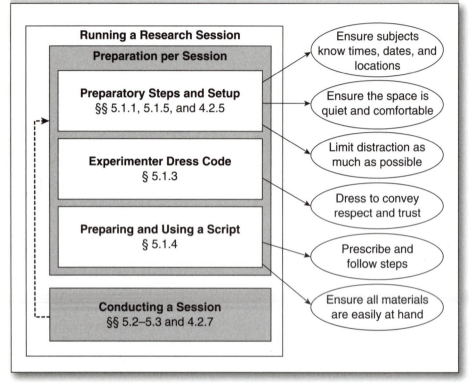

screen glare from overhead lights can be important—it may be helpful to use an incandescent table lamp instead of bright fluorescent ceiling fixtures. Allow for the possibility that some of your subjects may be left-handed—we have seen experimental setups that were very awkward for left-handers to use. In general, try to take the perspective of your subjects and make the setup as comfortable as possible for them.

In setting up the space, it is also important to consider possible distractions. For example, if your experimental space is next to an office or opens on a busy hallway, consider the possibility that loud conversations nearby may distract your subjects. The ideal setup for running individual subjects is a sound-isolated chamber or room, but such a space is not always available. A simple sign that reads "Experiment in Progress—Quiet Please" can help a great deal. If you must collect data in a room used for other purposes, such a sign can also help avoid accidental intrusions by others who may not realize an experiment is in progress. (Also, take the sign down after the study, or people in the building will learn to ignore it.) It is also best to remove "attractive nuisances"—objects that invite inspection—from the experimental space. For example, one of us collected data in a room that had a shelf full of toys and puzzles used in another study—until we found a subject playing with a puzzle rather than performing the experimental task!

Often, subjects may have to wait after arriving at your study, perhaps as other subjects finish. While you should try to minimize waiting time—unlike a doctor's office or driver's license center, your subjects don't *have* to be there—it is important to provide a comfortable place to wait. If the only waiting area available is a hallway, try at least to place chairs in an appropriate location with a sign that says "Please wait here for [TitleOfExperiment] experiment."

Figures 5.2 and 5.3 show two spaces used for running subjects in a psychology department. Figure 5.2 shows a small storage space used as a single-subject data-collection station. A table lamp is used to avoid glare from overhead fluorescent lights, and the room is kept free of distractions. The room is on a quiet, rarely used hallway, so this space provides good isolation. A nearby workroom serves as a reception and waiting area, as well as office space for research assistants. If there is not an easy way to watch the subjects through a one-way mirror, we have found video baby monitors to be helpful.

Figure 5.2.   A storage space used as a single-subject data-collection station.

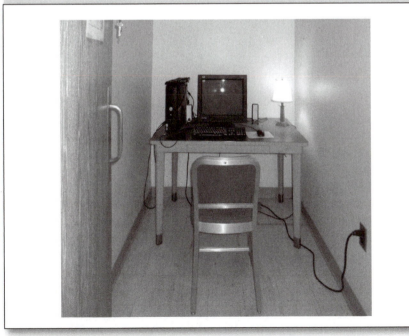

Figure 5.3.   An office space used to house multiple data-collection stations.

Figure 5.3 shows a large office used to house multiple data-collection stations. Office dividers separate the stations and provide some visual isolation while allowing a single experimenter to instruct and monitor several subjects simultaneously. In such setups, subjects are sometimes asked to wear headphones playing white noise to provide additional isolation. In this space, subjects wait for their sessions in the hallway, which also has a sign asking for quiet.

5.1.2 Piloting

As mentioned earlier, conducting a pilot study based on the script of the research study is important. Piloting can help you determine whether your experimental design "works." If a revision to the study is necessary, it is far better to find it and correct it before running multiple subjects, particularly when access to subjects is limited. It is helpful and far less stressful to think of designing experiments as an iterative process characterized by a cycle of design, testing, and redesign, as noted in Figure 1.1. In addition, you are likely to find that this process of running an experiment works in parallel with other experiments and may be informed by them (i.e., lessons learned from ongoing related lab work may influence your thinking).

Thus, we highly recommend that you use pilot studies to test your written protocols (e.g., the instructions for experimenters). The pilot phase provides experimenters the opportunity to test the written protocols with practice participants and is important for ironing out misunderstandings, discovering problematic features of the testing equipment, and identifying other conditions that might influence the participants. Revisions are a normal part of the process; do not hesitate to revise your protocols in consultation with the principal investigator (PI). This will save time later. There is also an art to knowing when not to change the protocol. Your PI can help judge this!

The major reason for returning to the topic of piloting is that the pilot study provides an opportunity to think through the issues raised here—the setup of the experimental space; interacting with subjects before, during, and at the conclusion of the experiment; and so on. Especially for an inexperienced experimenter, pilot testing provides an opportunity to practice all these things. In some cases, it may be effective to begin pilot testing with role-playing—one member of the research team plays the role of the subject, while another plays the role of experimenter.

You will often start piloting with other experimenters and then move to officemates and people down the hall. One researcher we know gets Institutional Review Board (IRB) approval early and switches to subjects that can be kept, using them as pilot subjects. When the process is smooth, this researcher declares them keepers. This is expensive, but for complicated studies is probably necessary because your lab mates know too much to be useful pilot subjects. It is important to keep in mind that once you involve actual subjects whose data you may keep, or who are recruited from a subject pool, all the issues concerning IRB approval discussed earlier come into play.

It is also important when piloting to test your data-gathering and analyses steps. We have wasted significant amounts of resources when the apparatus did not measure what we thought it did, and we know of numerous studies where the format of the study software output did not load easily and directly into analysis software or did not record the information that was later found to be needed. So, as an important part of piloting, take some of the pilot data and test-analyze them to see that the data are recorded cleanly and correctly, that they load into later analysis tools, and that the results you want to examine can be found in the recordings you have. You can also start to see if your manipulations are leading to changes in behavior.

5.1.3 Experimenter Dress Code

The goal of a dress code is to convey a serious atmosphere and to encourage respect and cooperation from your subjects. You should consider the impression you wish to make and will make when running your experiment.

This consideration should include how you wish to position yourself (in a way that commands respect while making the participants comfortable enough to perform the task), the type of experiment, and the type of participants in the experiment.

In most cases, we recommend wearing a semiprofessional outfit ("office casual"), such as a dress shirt with dress slacks, when running experiments. This helps you look professional and prepared but not intimidating. Semiprofessional dress helps convey the experiment's importance without overwhelming the participant. However, appropriate dress may vary depending on your subject population. If you are a college student interacting with college-student subjects, it may be best to dress like a college student—but think of a college student who wants to make a good impression on a professor, not a college student hanging out in the evening. It is certainly best to avoid things like T-shirts with slogans some might find offensive, low-cut blouses, very short shorts or skirts, or flip-flops. If you are working with non-student adult subjects, business casual is a better choice of dress. If your subjects are expert professionals, you should dress in a way that would fit their workplace.

5.1.4 Preparing and Using a Script

Your research study will likely have a script of how to run the session. If it does not, it should, because a script will help you run each subject in a confident and consistent manner. The script will often start with how to set up the apparatus. Before the subject's arrival, the experimenter needs to set up the apparatus and should be ready to welcome the subject. Incorrectly or inconsistently applied procedures cause inconsistencies in running the experiment (e.g., omission of an instruction resulting in noisier data). Consequently, the script that appropriately represents required procedures plays an important role in conducting a successful experimental study. Appendix 2 provides an example study script.

The setup should include making sure all materials that will be used in the session are available (e.g., forms, at least one backup copy) and that the apparatus is working. If batteries are used for any part of the apparatus (e.g., a laser pointer, a DVD remote), spare batteries should be on hand.

5.1.5 Before Subjects Arrive

Your interaction with the subjects you've recruited begins before they arrive. It is wise to remind subjects by phone or e-mail the day before a study is scheduled, if they have been scheduled farther in advance, and to repeat the time, place, and directions in the reminder. If there is a time window beyond which you cannot begin the study—for example, you might need to exclude from a group study anyone who arrives more than 5 minutes late—make sure this is clear as well.

As you schedule the times to run, you should take advice about when to schedule times. It is usually appropriate to schedule times during normal business hours (which in a university lab may be 10 a.m. to 6 p.m.). If you are running subjects outside of these normal hours you should have a discussion with the PI about safety for you and the subjects (how to reach the PI, for example). You should also consider practical issues such as whether the building will be locked after normal business hours or on weekends. If your subjects are traveling some distance to be in your experiments, do parking restrictions or bus schedules change after hours or on weekends?

It is also important to be clear about where the study is. Make sure that your subjects have clear directions to the location of your study. On a college campus, it may be important to provide directions and identify nearby landmarks. If subjects are driving to the location of your study, make sure you provide clear instructions on where to park and whether they are expected to pay for parking. Make sure the door to the building is unlocked, or have someone meet subjects at the door—one of us knows of an experiment in which several subjects were not run and hours of data collection were lost because the experimenter didn't realize the campus building would be locked after 5 p.m. and the subjects were literally lost.

You should also provide clear directions to the specific room in which the study is held. Several of us have seen research subjects wandering the halls looking for the room their experiment is in. It is also helpful to clearly mark the place where the experiment will be (or the place where subjects should wait)—a simple sign that says "Skill Acquisition Experiment here," for example, may save a lot of confusion in a building where all the halls and doorways look pretty much alike and where multiple experiments are in progress, or in buildings where the rooms are not numbered appropriately. If subjects must pass a receptionist to find your study, make sure the receptionist knows where the study is and who is running it—many people will stop to ask even if they think they know where they're going.

Making it as easy as possible for subjects to find your study and to arrive in a timely manner is important to ensure that they arrive ready to participate, with minimal anxiety. This helps in establishing the cooperative relationship with your subjects that will yield the best results for your experiment.

5.2 Running a Research Session

A research session will have roughly four phases: welcoming the subject, running the study itself, debriefing the subject, and then providing the subject with compensation when promised. Figure 5.4 provides a graphical overview of running a research session.

5.2.1 Welcome

As the experimenter, you are taking on a role similar to that of a host; thus, it is appropriate to welcome participants to the study. You might provide them reading materials if they have to wait and should answer any questions they have before the study begins. It is also appropriate to confirm their names (for class credit) and to confirm for them that they are in the right place at the right time. If the experimental protocol permits it, you might also indicate how long the study will take. This helps set the stage for the study itself.

The first event after welcoming subjects is typically the informed consent procedure. It is important to take this seriously—while it will become routine to you, it is likely not routine for your subjects. Rather than simply handing a subject the consent document and saying, "You have to sign this before we can start," take the time to explain the major points and to provide an opportunity for questions. Many will have no questions and will glance quickly at the document before signing it. Nevertheless, your approach every time should be one that allows the subject an opportunity to understand and think about what he or she is agreeing to.

5.2.2 Talking With Subjects

When you welcome the subjects to your study and the study area, you might feel uncomfortable in the first few sessions you run. After you have run a few sessions, this discomfort will go away. In a simple study, you can be quite natural, as there is nothing to "give away." In more complex studies, you will be busy setting up the apparatus, and this tends to make things less stressful for you. It is important, however, to realize that talking with subjects before they begin the experiment plays an important role in getting good data. Often, subjects come to the lab feeling nervous, with little or no experience participating in research and, perhaps, with misconceptions about the nature of behavioral research. For example, it is not unusual for students participating in university subject pools to believe that all experiments involve deception or that all researchers are surreptitiously evaluating their

Figure 5.4. A pictorial summary of running a research session, along with the section (§) or sections (§§) that explain each step.

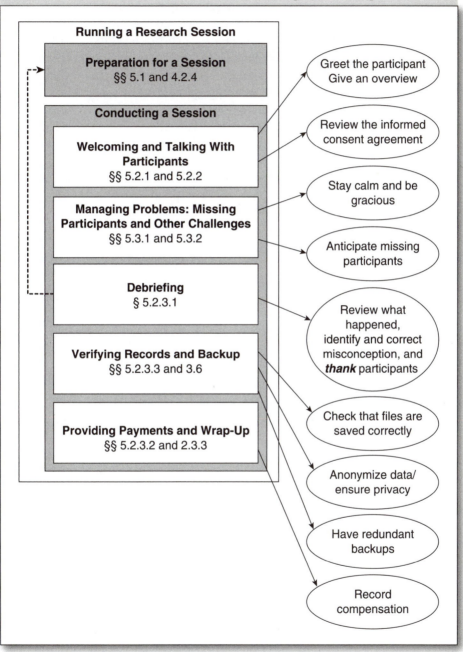

personalities or possible mental disorders. Interacting in a natural, cordial way and explaining clearly what your subjects will be asked to do can go a long way toward alleviating the subjects' anxiety and ensuring that they do their best to comply with the instructions and complete the experimental task. In our experience, it is all too easy for experimenters to interact with subjects in a rote and too remote manner that increases rather than alleviates their anxiety. Remember that although you may have repeated the experimental protocol dozens of times, it is the first time for each subject!

In nearly all cases, abstaining from extraneous comment on the study is an important and useful practice that makes all parties concerned more comfortable. Many experimental protocols require not giving the subject feedback during the study. In these cases, your notes will probably indicate that you tell the participants at the beginning of the session that you are not allowed to provide them feedback on their performance. Generally, the debriefing can handle most questions, but if you are not sure how to answer a question, either find and ask the PI or take the subject's contact information and tell him or her you will get an answer. And then do it! This also means that when you are running subjects for the first couple of times, someone who can answer your questions should be available.

In social psychology studies or where deception is involved, you will be briefed by the investigator and will practice beforehand. In this area, practice and taking advice from the lead researcher is particularly important.

Be culturally sensitive and respectful to the participants. Consult with the lead investigator if you have general questions concerning lab etiquette or specific questions related to the study.

There are a few things that seem too obvious to mention, but experience tells us that we should bring them up. Don't ask a subject for his or her phone number, no matter how attractive you find the subject! The experiment is not an appropriate context to try to initiate a romantic relationship. Don't complain about how hard it is to work in the lab or how difficult you found your previous subject. Don't tell a subject that his or her session is the last session of your workday, so you hope the session is over quickly. And so on. It might seem that nobody with common sense would do any of these things, but we've seen them all happen.

5.2.3 Concluding a Session

After your subject has finished participating in your experiment, several important parts of your interaction with him or her remain to be completed. These include debriefing, providing compensation, and checking the data.

It is also wise when concluding the experiment to make sure you have all the information you need from the subject. Do you have your copy of the consent document signed by the subject? Is information that will allow you to link pencil-and-paper data with computer data files properly recorded?

5.2.3.1 Debriefing

The American Psychological Association's ethical principles offer a general outline of debriefing procedures. For many experiments, the lead researcher may provide additional guidance. Experimenters should ensure that participants acquire appropriate information about the experiment—such as the nature, results, and conclusions of the research. If participants are misinformed on any of these points, investigators must take time to correct these misunderstandings. Also, if any procedures in a session are found to harm a participant, the research team must take reasonable steps to report and alleviate that harm.

Reviewing your plans for debriefing will be part of obtaining approval for your experiment from the IRB or ethics panel. Sometimes, there are local rules about debriefing—for example, a university subject pool may require a deeper educational debriefing for every study, even when the IRB does not. In an educational debriefing, you would describe the design of the study and the theoretical question it addresses in more detail, using keywords that allow the subjects to see connections between participating in your study and what they are learning in their classes. You may be required to provide a written debriefing or to have your debriefing approved by the administrator of your subject pool.

The experiment's procedures may cause participants to feel uncomfortable or alarmed (although this would be unusual). After the experiment is finished, investigators or experimenters should listen to the participants' concerns and try to address these problems. Mitchell and Jolley (2012) provided reasonable steps to follow when you debrief:

a. Correct any misconceptions participants might have.
b. Give a summary of the study without using technical terms and jargon.
c. Provide participants an opportunity to ask any questions they might have.
d. Express gratitude to the participants.

As with the informed consent procedure, you may find that some, even most, subjects are uninterested in the debriefing. Also, debriefing will become routine to you as you run more subjects. It is important not to let these things lead you to approach debriefing in a perfunctory way that conveys to all subjects that you do not consider it important. If only one subject appears interested, that is reason enough to take debriefing seriously.

As noted earlier, if your study has involved deception, you must usually reveal this deception to the subject. Even if there was no deception, it is good practice to spend a few minutes debriefing the subject about the purpose of the study—your hypotheses, how you hope to use the results, and so on. These are things you generally don't want to mention at the beginning of the experimental session but that will help your subjects understand the value of their participation.

When you have a study that can be perceived as being deceptive or when the study is a double-blind study, you should seek advice about how to debrief the participants. If deception is a procedural component, you will most likely have to explain this to the subject and ask that the subject not discuss the study until all the subjects have been run (after the study's completion date). For all studies, requesting that the subject refrain from discussing the study will help keep potential subjects from becoming too informed.

To review, double-blind studies prescribe that neither the subject nor the experimenter knows which treatment the subject has received. For example, the amount of caffeine a subject has ingested in a caffeine study with multiple possible doses would be revealed to the subject by a third party after the subject had left the experimenter, and this information would not be examined by the experimenters until all the subjects had been run. In these cases, you will have to explain the procedures of the study as well as provide a general rationale for double-blind trials. Otherwise, participants may balk at being given a treatment in a sealed envelope or by a person who is not the experimenter. Furthermore, events such as the Tuskegee experiment (see Chapter 3) underscore why procedural transparency is so essential.[1]

5.2.3.2 Payments and Wrap-Up

At the end of the session, you should be sure to compensate the subject as specified. Compensation can take the form of monetary payment, credit toward a class, or nothing. If you are paying subjects monetarily, check with your supervisor, as there are nearly always detailed instructions for how to process such payments. In any case, you should make sure that they receive their compensation, that you receive any required documentation back from them, such as receipts or signatures, and that you thank each participant for his or her assistance. Without the participants, after all, you cannot run the study.

---

[1]The abuses associated with these studies led to the Belmont Report and the modern IRB process as a means of mitigating future risks to experimental participants.

At the end of the wrap-up, you should set up for the next subject. Make sure that copies of forms are on hand and that, if you have used such things as spare batteries, you restock.

5.2.3.3 Verifying Records

After each subject, it is a good idea to make sure data files are properly closed. For example, if an EPrime program is terminated not by running to its normal conclusion but by shutting down the computer, the data file may not be saved correctly. Any paperwork, whether it contains data (e.g., a questionnaire) or simply clerical work (how much credit should be given) should be verified and appropriately filed.

This is also an appropriate time to anonymize the data, as discussed in Chapter 3. You will, of course, want to retain a record of subjects' names for purposes of assigning credit or documenting payment, but if it is not necessary to associate subject names with data, the names should be removed as soon as possible. Depending on the nature of the research, you may want to store a list of subject codes and names that could later be used to relink identity information with the data, but you should consider carefully whether this is necessary.

It is also useful to keep notes about every subject. For example, if something unusual happened—the subject reported an apparent problem with the experimental software, the subject seemed to ignore instructions, a loud distraction occurred in the hallway—this should be noted so that the lead researcher or PI can make a judgment about whether to include that subject's data, whether to conduct additional tests on the software, and so on. Don't think, "I'll remember to mention this at the lab meeting"—you won't, at least some of the time. One of us asks our research assistants to initial a list of subjects to verify that everything went smoothly, including entering the correct information in the program running the experiment, starting on time, and so on. Sometimes, too, a subject will say something that provides an insight into the research question—if that happens, write it down at the end of the session. Such insights can be like dreams: clear and vivid in the moment and impossible to remember later.

It is also useful to document, perhaps in a lab notebook, information such as the date when particular data were collected (the dates on data files may reflect when they were last accessed rather than when they were collected), the file names for programs used to collect data, and so on.

This advice may seem obsessive, but it comes from long experience in running experiments. It is likely that the experiment you are running is one of many conducted in the laboratory you're working in, and perhaps one of many that you're running yourself. Having a record you don't need is not a problem; lacking a record you do need may mean that the data collection effort was wasted or at least that you will need to spend a lot of time reconstructing exactly what you did.

5.2.4 Running Simulated Subjects

You may find yourself running simulated subjects. User models and simulations are increasingly used, both as stand-alone objects and sometimes as part of a study to provide a social context. For example, to model a social situation, you might have two intelligent agents act as confederates in a resource allocation game (Nerb, Spada, & Ernst, 1997). These agents provide a known social context in that their behavior is known and can be repeated, either exactly or according to a prescribed set of knowledge.

When you run simulations as subjects, you should keep good notes. There are often differences between the various versions of any simulation, and this should be noted. Simulations will also produce logs, and these logs should be stored as securely and accurately as subject logs. There may be more of them, so annotating them is very prudent.

If you create simulations, you should keep a copy of the simulation with the logs as a repeatable record of the results. You should perform enough runs that your predictions are stable (Ritter, Schoelles, Quigley, & Klein, 2011) and then not modify those files of model and runs but only copies of them.

Obviously, many of the issues discussed in this chapter do not apply to simulated subjects—no one, to our knowledge, has ever proposed that a simulated subject should be debriefed! Nevertheless, the importance of a clear protocol for your experiment is unchanged.

5.3 Other Issues

While running a session, issues may arise. Often these are negative, and you want to be prepared for them. Sometimes, however, you can learn something not anticipated.

5.3.1 Missing Subjects

Every study has two key parties—the experimenter and the subject or subjects (when running groups). Inevitably, you will encounter a situation where a participant does not show up, despite having an appointment. While participants should notify you in advance if they are going to be absent, keep in mind that missed appointments do happen, and plan around this eventuality. Subjects are participating voluntarily (even when they receive compensation)—nobody is required to participate in a particular experimental procedure. Therefore, it is appropriate to be gracious about absences. Where possible, we recommend offering to reschedule once. However, when there are repeated absences, it is often not worth rescheduling. Bethel and Murphy (2010) estimated that about 20% of subjects will fail to arrive. This seems slightly high to us; for example, in the Psychology Department subject pool at our university, the no-show rate is typically 5% to 7%. In any case, the lesson is that you will have to schedule more subjects than your target to reach your target number of subjects, particularly for repeated session studies, studies with groups, or populations with understandable difficulties.

In some cases, you as an experimenter may need to cancel an experimental session. It is unacceptable for an experimenter simply not to show up for a session. When you really have to cancel the experiment, you should do it in advance. Furthermore, as the experimenter, you should cancel a session by directly contacting the participants.

Note that in some cases, there will be specific rules about these issues—for example, the policies of your subject pool may require 24-hour notice to cancel an experimental session or may have criteria for when absence is excused or unexcused. It is important to know and follow these rules.

5.3.2 Other Problems and How to Deal With Them

Most cognitive psychology and human–computer interaction studies run smoothly. However, if you run experiments long enough, you will encounter problems—software crashes, apparatus breaks, power goes out, and so on. Sometimes, too, there are more person-oriented problems—difficult subjects or problems that involve psychological or physical risks to the subject. Ideally, the research team will have discussed potential problems in advance and developed plans for handling them. It is the nature of problems, though, that they are sometimes unanticipated.

The most common problems are minor—software or equipment failures, issues with materials, and so on. In responding to such problems, the most important things to remember are (a) remain calm—it's only an experiment—and (b) try to resolve the problem in a way that does not cause difficulties for your subject. For example, computer problems are often solved by rebooting the computer—but if this happens 30 minutes into a 1-hour session and you would have to start over at the beginning, it is not reasonable to expect the subject to extend his or her appointment by half an hour, nor would the data likely be usable. Often, the best thing to do is apologize, give the subject the compensation promised (after all, the subject made the effort to attend and the problem is not the subject's fault, and it is appropriate to be generous in these circumstances), make a note in the lab notebook, and try to fix things before the next subject appears.

It can be harder to deal with problems caused by difficult subjects. Sometimes, a subject may say, "This is too boring; I can't do this . . . ," or simply fail to follow instructions. Arguing with these subjects is both a waste of your time and unethical. As noted in Chapter 3, a basic implication of the voluntary participation is that a subject has the right to withdraw from a study at any time, for any reason, without penalty. Depending on the situation, it may be worthwhile to make one attempt to encourage cooperation—for example, saying, "I know it is repetitive, but that's what we have to do to study this question"—but don't push it. A difficult subject is unlikely to provide useful data, anyway, and the best thing is to end the session as gracefully as you can, note what went on, and discuss the events with the PI.

You can also encounter unexpected situations in which a participant is exposed to some risk of harm. For example, occasionally, a subject may react badly to an experimental manipulation such as a mood induction or the ingestion of caffeine or sugar. It is possible, though extremely rare, for apparatus to fail in ways that pose physical risks (e.g., if an electrical device malfunctions). And very rarely, an emergency situation not related to your experimental procedure can occur—for example, we know of instances in which subjects have fainted or had seizures while participating in experiments, and fire alarms can go off at any time.

Investigators must be committed to resolving these problems ethically, recognizing that the well-being of the participants supersedes the value of the study. If an emergency situation does arise, it is important that the experimenter remain calm and in control. If necessary, call for help. If the problem is related to the experimental procedure, it may be wise—or necessary—to cancel upcoming sessions until the research team has discussed ways to avoid such problems in the future.

It is important to bring problems and risks to the attention of the lead researcher or PI. In the event of problems that result in harm to subjects, it is important to consult the relevant unit responsible for supervising research, such as the IRB. These problems are called "adverse events" and must be reported to the IRB.

5.3.3 Chance for Insights

Gathering data can be tedious, but it can also be very useful. The process of interacting with subjects and collecting data gives you a chance to observe aspects of behavior that are not usually recorded, such as the subjects' affect, posture, and emotional responses to the task. These observations that go beyond your formal data collection can provide useful insights into the behavior of interest. Talking informally with subjects after they have finished the experiment can also provide insights. You may find that subjects did not understand some aspect of the instructions. This is shown in Figure 5.4, where insights from debriefing may provide feedback (shown with the dashed arrow) that alters the setup and running of a session.

Obtaining these kinds of insights and the intuition that follows from these experiences is important for everyone, but gathering data is particularly important for young scientists. It gives them a chance to see how previous data have been collected and how studies work. Reading will not provide you this background or the insights associated with it; rather, this knowledge comes only from observing the similarities and differences that arise across multiple subjects in an experiment.

So be engaged as you run your study and perform the analysis. These experiences can be a source for later ideas, even if you are doing what appears to be a mundane task. In addition, being vigilant can reduce the number and severity of problems that you and the lead investigator encounter. Often, these problems may be due to changes in the instrument or changes due to external events. For example, current events may change word frequencies for a study on reading. Currently, words such as *bank*, *stocks*, and *mortgages* are very common, whereas these words were less prevalent a few years ago. Billy Joel's song "We Didn't Start the Fire" highlights these changes.

5.4 Running the Low Vision HCI Study

The example studies again illustrate concepts in this chapter. Judy's study illustrates the importance of piloting and what can be learned about the apparatus during the pilot study. While starting to set up the pilot study, Judy identified the experiment's first major issue: The company's software was not cross-system compatible; that is, it did not run on all versions of Windows. This was useful information and helped refine the experimental setup and protocol.

During the pilot study, the two pilot subjects (who were legally blind and not part of the subject pool) identified persistent text-to-voice issues. The team was able to successfully implement a version of the software that was cross-system compatible for the experiment, but the text-to-voice issues could not be entirely eliminated within the time period allotted for the study.

These problems caused Judy to reconsider her test groups, adding two additional groups. Besides the control group (unmarked navigation bar) and the first experimental condition (marked navigation bar), she added two other experimental conditions: (a) a customizable graphical interface controlled with the arrow keys, without a marked navigation bar and (b) a customizable graphical interface with a marked navigation bar.

The decision to add a customizable graphical interface was in response to the text-to-voice issues—the company's text-to-voice processing had a difficult time with book and movie titles, particularly if those titles included numbers. A major component of Judy's experiment tested the software's ability to support users' browsing book and movie titles. The relative lack of surrounding text in these lists caused the software's hidden Markov models to frequently misread years as numerals. Because the software's statistical tools for disambiguating between differing pronunciations also largely depended on surrounding text, Judy's text-to-voice software would in some cases mispronounce words—for instance, failing to distinguish between the noun and verb forms of the word *project*. Consequently, in the pilot study, Judy was uncertain if the lag times associated with the original experimental conditions were, in fact, a result of the treatment or confusion caused by the text-to-voice issues.

To isolate to some extent the effects associated with the software, Judy's team implemented a customizable graphical interface that allowed users to increase the size of a selected object with the up-and-down arrow keys and the color with the left-and-right arrow keys.

5.5 Running the Multilingual Fonts Study

In this example, developing our discussion from Chapter 4 regarding internal validity, we specifically discuss piloting to improve internal validity. Through piloting, we often find procedural or methodological mistakes that have consequences for an experiment's internal and external validity.

In the initial pilot data, Ying discovered a distribution in the data that she could not initially explain. The effect of changes in pixel density and size matched her expectations (denser letters were generally clearer, as were larger ones, with the magnitude of these effects eventually flattening off). Also as expected, she did find a relationship between matrix formats and these thresholds when the participants encountered a black font on a white background. However, she found that her color findings, even for Roman characters, did not match the literature. Previous work had shown that not only a font's size and density but also its brightness difference has an influence on its readability, and that light text on dark backgrounds and dark text on light backgrounds have predictably different distributions. Ying and Edward's pilot data did not even remotely match the distributions found in the literature.

Ying, Edward, and the PI began brainstorming about the possible causes for this discrepancy. Looking through the pilot study's screening questionnaire, Edward noted that there were no questions regarding color-blindness. Further, the initial survey questions asked the participants to rank the matrix formats' colors relative to each other for formats of a given size and density. The initial list did avoid sequentially listing orange, red, and green matrix formats; however, it listed a blue matrix format followed by a yellow one. Many participants refused to complete the rankings because they could not see any distinguishable differences between the matrix format within a given size and density condition. Consequently, Ying's light-background/dark-font distribution was essentially bimodal and incomplete, where the bimodality was a result of whether the format was ranked or not.

To address this problem, Edward and Ying expanded the screening questionnaire to include questions about color-blindness. In addition, they replaced their relative ranking scale and replaced it with a Likert scale, where participants encountered each color for a given condition separately. They then could respond to the question, "Do you find this sentence easy to read?" by selecting one of five answers: strongly agree, agree, unsure, somewhat disagree, or disagree.

Summarizing the data required additional steps, because on this measure the relative emotional distance between selections cannot be assumed—the distance between *strongly agree* and *agree*, for instance, may be larger or smaller than that between *unsure* and *agree* for a given topic. So, for the purposes of summarizing the data, Ying had to group selections into positive and negative responses and then order the color format within a given pixel/density condition with respect to the number of positive or negative responses collected. Ying could then see the gradation in user preferences for the given brightness differences across the various matrix formats, both in the new pilot data and later in the study.

Piloting, in this case, led to a slightly different but better procedure. The data were slightly harder to analyze, but the data were cleaner, and color-blind subjects were not frustrated.

5.6 Running the HRI Study

The HRI (human–robot interface) study also illustrates issues that arise when running a study and resolution of those issues. A problem that Bob is very likely to find in running his study is that of recruiting suitable subjects.

Unlike universities, companies frequently do not have a lot of potential subjects available. Often, the only people readily available are those who know about the product or have a vested interest in seeing the product succeed commercially. These are not ideal subjects to test a robot. Bob will have to look into recruiting people through newspaper ads, casual contacts, and other contacts at and through the company.

When piloting his study, Bob found that the default video format for his camera did not match the video-editing tools. This was quickly and easily fixed by changing the video at the recording. Otherwise, it would have added a needless step. He also bought a large disk drive—two, actually: one to record to and one to store off-site—to back up his video recordings. (He was careful to encrypt the disk.)

In running his study in service of a company developing a product, Bob might find that he is tempted to terminate his study or controlled observation early when he finds useful results. Of all our examples, his study would be the most appropriate to terminate early because that is what he is looking for—changes that lead to a better product. He is not looking for a general answer to publish but is looking for results to improve his product. On the other hand, if the people he is trying to convince are skeptical, he may particularly want to finish the study because robots are hard to set up and maintain and more reports of subjects pounding the table in frustration may be more convincing. Similarly, if he finds dangerous conditions or results that are conclusive on an engineering level, he has an obligation to provide his feedback early and not put further subjects at risk.

5.7 Conclusion

Running the experiment is usually the culmination of a lot of work in developing the research question and hypotheses, planning the experiment, recruiting the subjects, and so on. It can also be the fun part, as you see your work coming to fruition and the data accumulate. There is a lot to attend to while running an experiment, but it is the last step before you have data to analyze and can find the answer to your research question.

5.8 Further Readings

Huck, S. W., & Sandler, H. M. (1979). *Rival hypotheses: Alternative interpretations of data based conclusions*. New York: Harper & Row.

This book provides a set of one-page case studies about how data can be interpreted and what alternative hypotheses might also explain the study's results. Following each case study is an explanation of what other very plausible rival hypotheses should be considered when interpreting the experiment's results. This book is engaging and teaches critical thinking skills for analyzing experimental data. It also reminds you of biases that can arise as you run studies. It would be useful as a reading for other chapters in the present text as well.

Mitchell, M. L., & Jolley, J. M. (2012). *Research design explained* (8th ed.). Belmont, CA: Wadsworth.

This book's appendix ("Online Practical Tips for Conducting an Ethical and Valid Study") offers useful tips similar to those in the present text.

5.9 Questions

Summary Questions

1. Describe the following terms.
   a. What is *debriefing*?
   b. List the procedures in debriefing, as noted by Mitchell and Jolly (2012).
   c. What is a *simulated subject*?
   d. What is an *adverse event*?
   e. What does *double-blind* refer to?

2. Consider where each of the example studies could be run in your environment, and draft a plan for doing so.

3. When can a subject decide to stop participating in a study?

Thought Questions

1. *Preparing a study.* Refer to the example scripts in Appendix 2. For your own study or one of the example studies, do the following:
   a. Prepare an experimental script.
   b. Prepare an informed consent form.
   c. Prepare a debriefing form.

2. Using only one figure or a similar, short (about 1-minute) task, prepare a short script to test the use of an ATM machine or logging into a computer. Run five people and note how you revised the script through using it.

3. Note how you would deal with the following potential problems in the study you are preparing or for one of the example studies:

a. a subject becoming ill during the study,

b. a subject getting lost and arriving 20 minutes late when another subject is scheduled to start in 10 minutes,

c. a subject coming in an altered state,

d. a subject self-disclosing that he or she has committed an illegal act on the way to the study,

e. a subject disclosing orally his or her private medical history,

f. a subject disclosing on a study form private medical history.

6

Concluding a Study

This chapter provides information about what you should do when you get done with your experiment. Figure 6.1 diagrams the several steps.

6.1 Data Care, Security, and Privacy

All information and data gathered from an experiment should be considered confidential. If others who are not associated with the experiment have access to either data or personal information, the participants' privacy could be violated. Thus, it is the responsibility of lead researchers and experimenters to ensure that all security assurance procedures are explained and enforced.

Researchers must safeguard against the inappropriate sharing of sensitive information. Personal information about the participants must not be shared with people not associated with the study. Thus, the data should not be left unattended. In most studies, experimental data are kept in locked files or on secure computers. The level of security may vary with the type of data. Anonymizing the data (removing personally identifying information) is a strong protection against problems. Anonymous reaction time data, where the only identifying information is a subject ID, is low or no risk. Personal health records, where the subjects might be identified by a combination of symptoms, are much more sensitive and require more cautious storage, perhaps being accessed only from a removable disk that is locked up when not in use.

Figure 6.1. A pictorial summary of concluding a research session and concluding a study, along with the section (§) or sections (§§) that explain each step.

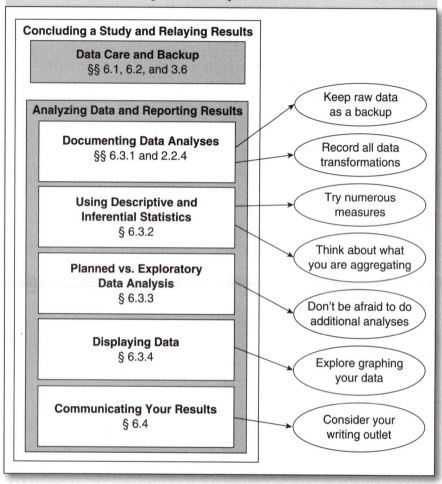

6.2 Data Backup

To protect against data loss, back up all your data routinely (after running a subject and every day when you are doing analyses of the data). If your data is stored in electronic files, keep them on a secure hard drive or burn them onto a CD. If you are using paper documents, they can be scanned and stored on a computer file as backup. We suggest that you back up your data after each subject while conducting a study, rather than backing up weekly.

6.3 Data Analysis

If you have planned your data collection carefully and pilot-tested your data collection and analysis plans, the data analysis stage of your experiment should be straightforward. However, there are often complications, especially if you are dealing with a complex data set with multiple independent and dependent variables, or complex measures such as verbal protocols. Even with carefully planned analyses, additional questions often arise that require further data analyses. If your research is submitted for publication, editors and reviewers may ask for additional analyses, which is only possible if your data are interpretable 1 month to 10 years later.

6.3.1 Documenting the Analysis Process

Our advice is to document the data analysis process very carefully. Many, perhaps most, experiments will require that you transform the data to analyze it. For example, if you have within-subjects variables, you will usually need to aggregate and transform the data so that levels of your independent variable are represented as columns rather than the rows likely to be in your data file. These transformations may be done in the program you use for analysis (e.g., SPSS) or in a spreadsheet program such as Excel. Always work from copies and keep careful notes on the steps of transformation, and never—never!—directly modify or discard the original, untransformed data files. If you filter your data to remove subjects who didn't follow instructions, outlying data points, or similar concerns and corrections, keep a record of exactly what you did and the names of filtered and unfiltered data files.

We find it is often useful to summarize your results as you work through the data analyses. The goal of data analysis is not to work through statistical procedures mechanically but, rather, to understand your data set and what it can tell you. It is useful to look not just at means—though differences in means may be the most important for your hypotheses—but at the actual distributions of data, how much they vary, and so on. Experienced researchers learn how to evaluate their data and analyses for plausibility—if something seems "off," it might be due to anomalous data (perhaps caused by a subject not taking the task seriously, an error in data entry, etc.), an error in manipulating the data file, or some other study-related reason. Thinking about whether the results of your analysis make sense and understanding how problems with the data can be responsible for odd results in your analysis is important.

Your data analysis will likely result in a number of output files. While most statistical software provides output that will let you trace exactly what you did to generate the output, doing so can be time-consuming. Keeping good notes of what is in each output file is likely to save time in the long run.

6.3.2 Descriptive and Inferential Statistics

Your data analysis will include two kinds of statistics: descriptive and inferential. Descriptive statistics are those that, as the name suggests, *describe* your data. Means and other measures that show the average or typical value of your data, standard deviations and other measures that show the variability of your data, and correlations and regressions that show the relations among variables are all descriptive statistics. Statistics texts will define a variety of descriptive measures, and statistical software will calculate many measures. When you are working with your own data, you will come to understand how important the choice of descriptive statistics can be. Does the mean really reflect the typical value of your data? Is the standard deviation misleading because your data include many extreme data points? The decisions you make about descriptive statistics are choices about the best way to summarize your data, both for your own thinking and to communicate to others. And, remember, descriptive statistics are both computed and reported first.

Detailed advice on choosing descriptive statistics is beyond the scope of this book. However, we can offer some practical advice: Explore the possible descriptive statistics so you get to know your data set. We have often seen researchers who missed or misconceived aspects of their data because they failed to consider a variety of ways to summarize them. Considering multiple graphic depictions of your data can be very useful. For example, looking at a distribution of response times may immediately show that the mean is not a good representation of the typical response time, perhaps suggesting that the median, which is less sensitive to extreme values, or a transformed version would be a better description. Graphing means, especially in factorial experiments that might reveal interactions among variables, can visually communicate trends that are difficult to see in a table of means. One of us has several times had the experience of regraphing an interaction that a research assistant thought was uninterpretable and immediately finding a simple and meaningful description of the interaction.

A particular issue that arises in describing data results from aggregating data over subjects. Of course we want to know what is common in the performance of all our subjects (within an experimental condition) taken together. Sometimes, though, averaging over subjects results in a misleading picture of what actually happened (e.g., Siegler, 1987). A common example with important theoretical and practical implications concerns learning curves observed in studies of skill acquisition. For many skills, performance as measured by response time improves with practice following a *power function,* such that performance speeds up very quickly over the first few trials of practice, then continues to speed up more slowly with additional trials (e.g., Bryan & Harter, 1897; Crossman, 1959; Ritter & Schooler, 2001; Seibel, 1963). Newell and his colleagues (Rosenbloom & Newell, 1987) were so impressed by this finding that they proposed the *power law of practice* as a basic phenomenon of skill acquisition. However, other researchers have pointed out that a power function for speedup can result from averaging over subjects, none of whom individually show such a speedup. For example, if each subject discovers a strategy that results in a dramatic, sudden, single-trial speedup but individual subjects discover the strategy after different numbers of trials, the average may suggest a gradual, power-function speedup displayed by no individual subject (Brown & Heathcote, 2003; Delaney, Reder, Staszewski, & Ritter, 1998; Estes, 1956).

Table 6.1 and Figure 6.2 illustrate this point using hypothetical data. Imagine subjects learning to perform a simple task that takes 1,000 seconds (about 17 minutes) to complete, until you find a shortcut that allows you to complete the task in half the time (500 seconds). If subjects vary in when they discover the shortcut, as illustrated in Table 6.1, averaging response-time data over subjects will generate the data points displayed in Figure 6.2. The dashed line shows the best-fitting power function for these data points. Examining the graph suggests that learning is a smooth, continuous process with a power-law speedup over trials. However, the actual process for each subject is a sudden discovery of a shortcut, resulting in a sharp, step-function speedup in performance. Thus, the averaged data obscures the true form of learning.

Of course, you want not just to describe your data but also to draw conclusions from it. This is where *inferential* statistics come into play. Again, detailed discussion of the many possible inferential statistics is beyond the scope of this book. However, we can offer a few pieces of practical advice. The first is to make sure that the statistics you choose are appropriate for your data and your research question. Many researchers have learned to use analysis of variance (ANOVA) as their primary analysis tool. However, when independent variables are on interval or ratio scales (see Chapter 2), regression analyses and their associated inferential statistics may be much more powerful. For example, it has become common in several areas of psychology to use working memory capacity as an independent variable, dividing subjects into those with high and low (above or below the median) capacity. ANOVA *can* be applied to such data but does not provide the most powerful test of whether and how working-memory capacity affects the dependent variable.

Table 6.1. Response time in seconds by learning trial (hypothetical data). Italics indicate the first trial after discovering a shortcut; bold indicates the trials before discovering a shortcut.

Subject	*Learning Trial*							
	1	*2*	*3*	*4*	*5*	*6*	*7*	*8*
1	**1,000**	*500*	500	500	500	500	500	500
2	**1,000**	*500*	500	500	500	500	500	500
3	**1,000**	*500*	500	500	500	500	500	500
4	**1,000**	*500*	500	500	500	500	500	500
5	**1,000**	*500*	500	500	500	500	500	500
6	**1,000**	**1,000**	*500*	500	500	500	500	500
7	**1,000**	**1,000**	*500*	500	500	500	500	500
8	**1,000**	**1,000**	*500*	500	500	500	500	500
9	**1,000**	**1,000**	**1,000**	*500*	500	500	500	500
10	**1,000**	**1,000**	**1,000**	**1,000**	*500*	500	500	500
11	**1,000**	**1,000**	**1,000**	**1,000**	**1,000**	*500*	500	500
12	**1,000**	**1,000**	**1,000**	**1,000**	**1,000**	**1,000**	*500*	500
Mean	1,000	791	667	625	583	542	500	500

Figure 6.2. Mean response time as a function of trial, with power law fit (data from Table 6.1; left) and the individual learning curves (right) superimposed on the average response time.

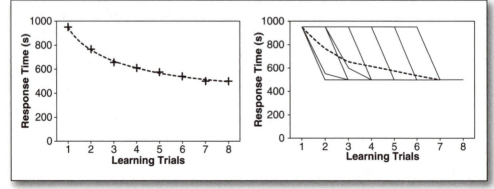

A second piece of advice is not to fall in love with a particular description of your data until you know that inferential statistics support your interpretation. Contrary to what some researchers think, inferential statistics do not draw your conclusions for you—instead, they tell you which of your conclusions are actually supported by the data. Third, and finally, don't fall into the trap of null-hypothesis reasoning—believing that the failure to find a significant difference is equivalent to finding evidence that there is no difference. Many research articles have been rejected for publication in part because a researcher argued that there was a meaningful difference in performance in one case and equivalent performance in another, when the statistical tests simply fell closely on either side of the conventional criterion for statistical significance.

6.3.3 Planned Versus Exploratory Data Analysis

If you have followed the advice in this book, you planned your data analyses well in advance. If that planning was successful, following the plan should provide the answers to your research questions and evidence for or against your hypotheses. However, most data sets are complex enough to allow additional analyses that are exploratory rather than planned. For example, your main question may be which of two experimental conditions resulted in greater accuracy. However, your data may allow you to explore the question of whether subjects' performance was more variable in one condition than another, or whether their performance depended on the order in which they solved problems (even though counterbalancing meant that order did not affect the test of your main hypothesis). Exploratory data analyses are often the source of additional insights into the research question or the basis of ideas for additional experiments, as a type of piloting the next study.

6.3.4 Displaying Your Data

If you are analyzing data, you will eventually need to communicate your results to someone—perhaps to the principal investigator (PI) supervising your research, colleagues at a conference, or the editors and reviewers (and, one hopes, the readers) of a journal. The diversity of possible research results makes it difficult to give general advice, but during the data analysis stage, we have one important suggestion: Make pictures early and often. A graph can make features of your data that are hard to extract from a data analysis output file stand out. If you have data that can be graphed in more than one way, do so. Modern software tools make it easy to generate graphs, and graphs are usually a much more efficient way to communicate your results— even to yourself—than are tables or lists of means.

6.4 Communicating Your Results

Rarely do people run experiments only for their own information. Instead, one of the goals is usually to communicate the results to others. In this section, we discuss some considerations about sharing your results based on having run a study.

6.4.1 Research Outlets

The written product resulting from your research project may take several forms. The simplest, a *technical report,* is usually written primarily as a report to the research sponsor. A technical report may be a final summary of a project or may serve as a progress report on an ongoing project. Technical reports are often written in a format specified by the research sponsor.

Another possibility is a presentation at a scientific conference. Such presentations may take several forms. One form is a talk, usually accompanied by slides prepared with PowerPoint, Keynote, Prezzi, or similar software. A typical conference talk is 10 to 20 minutes in length, followed by a brief question-and-answer session. Another kind of conference presentation is a poster. At a poster session, there are dozens, or sometimes hundreds, of posters in a large hall of some kind, with poster authors standing at their posters to discuss their research with individuals who stop by. Conference presentations can be very useful for getting feedback on your research, which can be helpful in preparing an article for publication or planning future experiments. Sometimes conference presentations are accompanied by brief papers published in the proceedings of the conference.

Often, the final product of a research project is an article in a scientific journal. Scientific journals are a means by which researchers in a field communicate with one another, including with future researchers For researchers employed in—or aspiring to—academic settings, a journal article is usually the most valuable product for advancing a career. A major benefit of publishing research in a scientific journal is that it will be available for other researchers. Scientific journals are typically quite selective in choosing articles to publish; some reject as many as 90% of the articles submitted for publication. Frequently, however, an initial rejection is accompanied by an invitation to revise and resubmit the article for reconsideration, or by suggestions for additional data collection to increase the value of the research to the field.

Students sometimes ask us if researchers are paid for articles published in scientific journals—the answer is, no, they are not, except on very rare occasions. (Journal publication does, however, often lead to higher salaries [Tuckman & Leahey, 1975].)

Reporting research results at a conference or in a scientific journal involves some form of *peer review*. This means that an editor or a conference program committee receives comments from several researchers with expertise in the area of research (peers) and uses those comments to decide whether to accept the proposed presentation or article. For a conference, the reviewers may consider a brief summary of the presentation or a more complete paper to be published in conference proceedings. The peer review process can seem quite daunting, but if you take the comments of reviewers as feedback on how to improve your research or your presentation of the research, you will nearly always find the comments quite helpful.

Choosing an outlet for your research will depend on several factors. Technical reports are usually mandated by the grant or contract that serves as an agreement with the research sponsor. A conference presentation may be an appropriate outlet for exploratory or partially completed research projects that are not yet ready for scientific journals—"works in progress" are appropriate for many conferences but usually not for scientific journals. Decisions about outlets are usually made by the lead researcher or PI, but it is in your interest to engage and learn about this process early.

Regardless of the outlet used to communicate your results, it is important to adjust your writing to the specific goals of and audience for the outlet. A technical report, for example, may have as its audience employees of the research sponsor who are not themselves researchers, and a primary goal may be recommendations concerning the practical implications of the research. The audience for a conference presentation is usually researchers working on similar topics, and the presentation should be developed with that audience in mind. A short conference talk or a poster makes efficiency of communication very important, and your goals may include having people remember your main message or making clear the aspects of the research for which feedback would be helpful. The audience for a journal article also includes researchers in related fields, so it is useful to keep in mind both the general style of the journals you have in mind and your own experience as a reader of journal articles.

6.4.2 The Writing Process

Guidance on writing research reports is beyond the scope of this book, but the *Publication Manual of the American Psychological Association* (APA, 2010) describes the standard format for preparing manuscripts for publication in psychological journals and offers some guidance on writing. We can say that if you have followed the advice in this book about preparing to run your study and keeping records, you will find yourself well prepared to begin writing.

One practical piece of advice we have concerning writing is this: Do not expect the first—or second or third—draft of your research report to be final. Members of a research team will pass drafts of research reports back and forth, and it is not unusual for there to be five, six, or even more drafts of a paper before it is submitted to a journal (this book got to Draft 54). And once an article is submitted to a journal, it will almost certainly have to be revised in response to comments from the editor and reviewers.

We have found that the amount of rewriting is often difficult for students to appreciate—they are used to submitting class papers after one or two drafts. One consequence of this is that student researchers are often reluctant to share their early drafts with others, including advisers or PIs. This is a mistake. Our best advice to student researchers is to share your work early and often, with anyone who is willing to read it and provide comments. Your goal should be to communicate your research effectively and to get feedback, not to impress others with your ability to produce a polished, finished product on the first try.

6.5 Concluding the Low Vision HCI Study

As Judy did the analyses and wrote up a short report summarizing the study, she found that the marked navigation bar with the customizable interface had the lowest lag times for the majority of users, followed by the customizable interface with an unmarked navigation bar and the marked navigation bar with no customizable interface. As expected, the control condition had the longest lag times. Creating plots of this helped her visualize and communicate these results. The study's small sample size made it impossible to determine if the marked navigation bar had a reliable effect for participants unable to detect changes in color or size ($n = 1$). For participants able to distinguish size or color to some extent ($n = 31$), the difference between the control group and fourth condition (the combination of a customizable interface and a marked navigation bar) was statistically significant, indicating that marked navigation bars do have a complementary effect. The differences between the other three conditions followed the expected trend but were not statistically significant.

The question of software remains. With better software, the relative differences between the four conditions might differ. Regardless, we would expect the lag times to decrease. As for the marked navigation bar's impact on performance for participants with virtually no visual acuity, Judy will need to find more participants. In addition, future studies are necessary to see if these trends translate to portable devices. E-readers and tablets are only now beginning to routinely support text-to-voice processing. Yet both devices are important new markets for her company.

To conclude, Judy's experiment is not unusual. Her study uncovered important trends but requires further studies to fully understand and extend these findings. Nevertheless, Judy's findings can be usefully incorporated in future products.

6.6 Concluding the Multilingual Fonts Study

Edward and Ying's experiences provide some insights for both concluding study sessions and concluding studies. Also, they provide an example of how to skillfully transition a technical report required for grant stakeholders into a conference paper.

The diverse cultural backgrounds and experiences of the study's participants made debriefing more important than is sometimes the case in human–computer interaction (HCI) studies. In many cases, participants from outside the immediate university community volunteered to participate in the study because of the study's similarity to the OLPC (One Laptop Per Child) project. While compensated, they nevertheless often did this at the cost of some personal discomfort, coming to a new place and interacting with people in a nonnative language. Frequently, their reading comprehension far exceeded their verbal fluency, making the experiment easy to complete but getting to the experiment and understanding the initial instructions more difficult. In this case, debriefing provided a way not only to go over what happened in the experiment but also to thank the participants and show how their participation was contributing to an important goal—global literacy.

Like most studies, Ying and Edward's study highlighted new research questions, as well as contributing new findings. Ying and Edward did find reliable differences in the preferences of users across the experimental conditions. As expected, they also found that users generally preferred darker fonts on lighter backgrounds.

On the other hand, there are further questions. For instance, while this study suggested that 8-x-8 formats were preferable, the pedagogical literature suggests that children respond more favorably to greater brightness differences than do most adults. This work, however, has generally occurred in the United States. Other studies (Al-Harkan & Ramadan, 2005) suggest that color preferences at least seem to be culturally relative. Therefore, testing the generalizability of the findings from the pedagogical literature and how they might inform user interface design for users of inexpensive laptops requires more studies. Ying had considered this problem early in the experimental design process after uncovering these findings during the literature review, but when recruiting proved to be difficult, Ying and her adviser realized that recruiting enough child participants to answer this question would be infeasible. Noting in the discussion sections of both the technical report and conference paper the need for this follow-up study, Ying proposed an on-site or web-based study at various user locations, especially because the screen resolution would already be consistent and this research question seems to entail fewer environmental controls.

Moving this work from a technical report to a conference paper was a relatively simple process with respect to writing new content, with the most difficulty associated with focusing the presentation on a few key ideas. Initially, Edward had a difficult time identifying and summarizing key procedural details. Allowing Ying and the PI to see his incomplete, fragmentary work was a difficult process for him. Fortunately, by this time, Edward trusted Ying enough to submit these ugly drafts and take advice from her on his writing. Looking back, having the tech report in hand made writing far easier.

Nevertheless, learning to work through multiple drafts (including updating the date and version number for each draft), managing references, and finding a weekly meeting schedule that met everyone's needs required some patience and negotiation. In our experience, we find these are common problems for undergraduate and graduate students working on their first few publications. Have patience and take the advice of your coauthors with an untroubled heart—there will be a lot of revisions, but they are a normal part of the process.

6.7 Concluding the HRI Study

Some aspects of Bob's work influenced how to wrap up his study. The first is the nature of the audience for his results. Bob should find out the norms and styles of result summaries that will influence the engineers and managers the most and provide the results to them in these formats. This may include a choice of what is reported (speed, accuracy, satisfaction), may be in the format of a short e-mail, may be a short tech report, and may in some cases be edited videos of subjects' experiences using the robot. He should keep in mind that his goal is to improve the product and to present his results in ways that are easy for the engineers to understand and act on (Kennedy, 1989).

The second assumption is that he may not be the person to make use of the data at a later time. As Bob wraps up his study, he should be careful to anonymize his results so that the privacy of his subjects will remain protected. He should back up his data and annotate it clearly enough that it can be reused. He should label his results, either with paper in a folder or in a computer file associated with the data and analyses files. He should, with the time allowed to him, document what he did and what he found. He should archive shareable data as best he can at the company, perhaps in a company library if there is one, or with his manager and the technology developer. The more private data, such as video recordings, should be stored in a safe place. In some ways, his results will come out as a report like those in the other example projects, because that style of report is useful and such reports will make the data and results more understandable across time and distance.

Bob particularly needs to keep in mind how to be persuasive. An article in *The Psychologist* summarized it well: "The best chance of changing the minds of the non-believers would be an artful combination of clear, strong logical argumentation mixed with value-affirming frames and presented in a humble manner that produces positive emotional reactions" (Munro, 2011, p. 179). So Bob must make his argument for changes clearly, using the values and ethics shared by the company (e.g., acknowledging the technical achievement and also noting the costs for change); this also means writing well, broadly defined to include well-done and appropriate figures and formatting in a style the readers expect.

6.8 Conclusion

As we discussed in Chapter 1, finishing an experiment is usually not the end of the research process. Often, the results will lead to new or refined research questions; better experimental tasks, designs, or procedures; or all these. Nevertheless, there is great satisfaction in completing an experiment and seeing the results. This is the payoff, and it is important to make sure that you wrap things up effectively.

6.9 Further Readings

There are few materials on how to run a study session or complete a study but plenty on how to analyze your data and communicate your results.

Howell, D. C. (2008). *Fundamental statistics for the behavioral sciences* (6th ed.). Belmont, CA: Thompson Wadsworth.

This is one of several good, commonly used statistics books.

Huff, D., & Geis, I. (1993). *How to lie with statistics*. New York: W. W. Norton.

> This, and earlier versions, discuss how to interpret results and report them. It is also relatively amusing and easy to read.

Sanderson, P. M., & Fisher, C. A. (1994). Exploratory sequential data analysis: Foundations. *Human-Computer Interaction, 9*(3–4), 251–317.

> Sanderson and Fisher introduce the idea of exploring the temporal structure of sequential data. This can help you see patterns in your data that simple means don't address.

Strunk, W., & White, E. B. (1979). *The elements of style*. New York: Macmillan.

> No matter the edition, this is a timeless first book on how to improve writing.

Tukey, J. W. (1977). *Exploratory data analysis*. New York: Addison-Wesley.

> Tukey introduces the idea of exploring your data. This can help you see patterns in your data that simple means don't address.

6.10 Questions

Summary Questions

1. Describe the following terms:
   a. *descriptive* and *inferential statistics*
   b. *table* and *figure*
   c. *exploratory data analysis*

2. How does running experimental sessions provide you with a "chance for insights"? Can you think of or find an example of this happening?

3. In completing your research study, the final product can be such a thing as an article in a journal or conference. Reporting results may involve a form of *peer review*. Describe these types of outputs, give an example of each, and describe what peer review is.

4. Describe your lab notebook and how you use it.

Thought Questions

1. The importance of data backup in conducting a research study with subjects cannot be overemphasized. Discuss how you plan to back up your data.

2. In an ideal world, where would you suggest that the researchers in the three examples (low vision HCI study, multilingual fonts study, and HRI study) publish their work?

3. Describe your work with a one-paragraph abstract. Note three possible venues to publish your work.

4. Do peer reviews in your class by sharing the paragraph abstracts and having the reviews organized by your teacher. What lessons can the class learn through sharing the reviews?

Afterword

There are many books available concerning research methods and related statistical analyses. We realized, however, that students usually have few opportunities to learn and practice the implicit knowledge associated with running their own experiments, and there are no books that we are aware of that either formalize or teach students about these practical considerations (e.g., preparing experimental environments and scripts, coordinating participants, or managing data, etc.).

Students charged with running experiments frequently lack specific domain knowledge regarding experimental methods. Consequently, young researchers chronically make preventable mistakes. With this book, we hope to provide practical knowledge about running experiments for students and industrial researchers. The topics and guidance contained in this book arise from the authors' collective experience in both running experiments and mentoring students.

To summarize, the book covered four major topics. *First, we discussed how to run a study safely.* This included how to recruit participants ethically and methods for minimizing risks to participants and experimenters.

Second, we discussed experimental repeatability and validity. We described methods for ensuring repeatability so that others can replicate and validate your work. For example, we described how to present the same experience to each subject across every session (and how to minimize differences between study sessions). This is an important aspect of being able to replicate and interpret the data. We also discussed strategies for mitigating risks, such as experimenter or demand effects that might jeopardize the uniformity of this experience.

Third, we discussed how to potentially gain further insights from the experimental process. These insights may or may not be outside the strict bounds of your experiment, but in either case, they can lead to new and often very productive work. We described approaches to piloting, debriefing, and data analysis that make further insights more likely, and we provided anecdotal examples of these approaches in action. You may not be able to examine all of the insights with the study you are running, but you can analyze many of them in later studies.

Fourth, we discuss recording data and reporting results. The process of setting up and running the study is to learn something new and to *share* it. The work is not completely done until it is published. Some publications can come much later than we might anticipate or prefer, so documentation of the steps and what the data and analyses are will help with this payoff. We discuss matching study goals to publishing goals, including the potential ramifications of publishing goals for the Institutional Review Board process. Examples of the forms you will need are provided in the appendices.

Stepping back for a moment, we recognize that further methods of gathering, analyzing, and visualizing data are being developed. Though these changes will impact the development of future experimental procedures, the gross structures of a study and the aspects we have discussed here (piloting, scripts, anonymizing data, etc.) are unlikely to change.

As you venture into research, you will find new topics that will interest you. In this text, we are unable to examine all the populations or touch on all the measures and tools necessary for exploring research questions in cognitive science, human factors, human–computer interaction, or human–robot interaction. Consequently, we are not able to cover in detail the collection of eye tracking, biological specimens, or functional magnetic resonance imaging. Nevertheless, we believe this book will allow you to anticipate many of the risks associated with research design and implementation in these areas. In essence, we believe you will ask the right questions that will allow you to successfully run studies using these techniques, when supplemented by further reading, consultation with colleagues, and practice.

Running studies is often exciting work, and it helps us understand how people think and behave. It offers a chance to improve our understanding. We wish you good luck, *bonne chance,* as you endeavor to learn and share a little bit more about the world.

Appendix 1

A Checklist for Preparing Studies

This checklist contains high-level steps that are nearly always necessary for conducting studies with human participants. As an experimenter or a principal investigator for your project, you need to complete the tasks below to set up a study. You might use this list verbatim, or you might modify it to suit your study. The list is offered in serial order, but work might go on in parallel or in a different order.

☐	Identify research problems and priorities, design study
☐	Prepare the Institutional Review Board form and submit it to the office of research protection, noting how to address any harm or risks
☐	Prepare "consent form"
☐	Prepare "debriefing form"
☐	Set up the study environment
☐	Run pilot tests to check your experimental design and apparatus
☐	Analyze pilot study data
☐	Prepare study script
☐	Receive Institutional Review Board approval
☐	Advertise the study and recruit participants (e.g., a flyer, a student newspaper)
☐	Run the study (Make sure a lab for the study is available for when you need to run) • Explain the study to participants (e.g., purpose, risk, benefits) • Gather data and store data
☐	Report results

Appendix 2

Example Scripts for Running Studies

A2.1 A High-Level Script for a Human–Computer Interaction Study

This is an example high-level summary script for an experiment. While experiments and controlled observations will differ across types and across studies, this script includes many common elements. It was used for Kim's (2008) PhD thesis study and has been slightly revised.

Experimenter's Guide

Every experimenter should follow these procedures to run our user study about skill retention.

1. Before you come to the lab, dress appropriately for the experiment. [Also see section 5.1.3 covering the role of a dress code.]

2. Before your participants arrive, you need to set up a set of the experiment apparatus.

    a. Start RUI (Recording User Input) in the Terminal Window. (See details below.)
    b. Start the Emacs text editor.
    c. Prepare disposable materials and handouts, such as the informed consent form.
    d. Turn on the monitor located in the experimental room so that you can monitor the participant outside the room.

3. Welcome your participants when they arrive.

4. Put a sign on the door indicating that you are running subjects when the experiment starts.

5. Give the Institutional Review Board approved consent form to the participants and have them read it.

6. If they consent, start the experiment.

7. Briefly explain what they are going to do.

8. Give them the study booklet.

   Participants can use 30 min. maximum to study the booklet.

9. While participants are reading the booklet, you can answer their questions about the task.

10. When the session is finished, give an explanation about the payment or extra credit. Thank them; give them a debriefing form. Also, if there are any additional sessions, remind them.

11. Take down the sign on the door when the experiment is done.

12. Copy the data to the external hard drive.

13. Shut down the apparatus.

14. Prepare supplies for the next subject.

Using RUI

RUI will be used to log keystrokes and mouse actions of the participant. RUI requires Mac OS X 10.3 (Panther) or later versions. It has been tested up to Mac OS X 10.5.8 (Snow Leopard). For RUI to record user inputs, "Enable access for assistive devices" must be enabled in the Universal Access preference pane. To start RUI:

1. Launch Terminal.

2. In Terminal, type the below information:
   "./rui –s "SubjectID" –r ~/Desktop/ruioutput.txt"

3. You will get this message: "rui: standing by—press ctrl+r to start recording . . ."

4. Press "CTRL+r"

5. To stop recording, press "CTRL+s"

Note: If you see the message "-bash: ./rui: Permission denied" in the Terminal window, you need to type "chmod a+x rui" while you are in the RUI directory.

A2.2 A More Detailed Script for a Cognitive Psychology Experiment

This script, slightly revised, was used in conducting an experiment reported in Carlson and Cassenti (2004).

1. Access the names of participants from the subject pool. Go to subject pool under "favorites" in Explorer, type in experiment number 1013 and password ptx497. Click on the button labeled "view (and update) appointments." Write down the names of participants on the log sheet before they start arriving.

2. Turn on computers in the subject running rooms if they aren't already on. If a dialog box comes up asking for you to log in, just hit cancel.

3. As participants arrive, check off their names on your list of participants. Make sure they are scheduled for our experiment—sometimes students go to the wrong room.

4. Give each participant two copies of the informed consent form (found in the wooden box under the bulletin board). Make sure they sign both copies and you sign both copies. Make sure to ask if the participant has ANY questions about the informed consent form.

5. Fill out the subject running sheet with subject's FIRST name only, handedness (right or left), gender, the room in which he or she will be run, and your name.

6. Begin the experiment by clicking on "simple counting" file on desktop. Once the program opens, press F7. Enter the subject number from the subject running sheet. When it asks for session number, you should always enter "1." Double-check the information when the confirmation box comes up. If the next screen asks you if it's okay to overwrite data, click "no" and put in a different subject number, changing the experiment sheet as needed. If you want to do all this while the participant is reading the informed consent to save time, go right ahead, but make sure to answer any informed-consent–related questions the participant may have.

7. Take the participant to the room and say the following: **"This experiment is entirely computerized, including the instructions. I'll read over the instructions for the first part of the experiment with you."** Read the instructions on the screen verbatim. Ask if the participant has any questions. After answering any questions the participant may have, leave the room and shut the door behind you. Place the "Experiment in Progress" sign on the door.

8. At two points during the experiment, subjects will see a screen asking them to return to Room 604 for further instructions. When they come out, you can lead them back to the room, taking along the paper for Break #1 and a pen. Read aloud to them the instructions printed on the top of the sheet and ask if they have any questions. Give the participants 2 minutes to work on their list, then come back in and press the letter *g* (for "**go on**"). This will resume the experiment where they left off. Ask again if they have any questions, then leave the room again and allow them to resume the experiment. The second time the subject returns to 604, follow the same procedure, this time with the instructions and paper for Break #2.

9. Fill out the log sheet if you haven't done so. You should have the necessary information from the subject pool. If somebody is signed up but doesn't show up, fill out the log sheet for that person anyway, writing "NS" next to the updated column.

10. Fill out a credit slip for each participant, and be sure to sign it.

11. Update participants on the web. Anyone who doesn't show up (and hasn't contacted us beforehand) gets a no-show. People who do show up on time should be given credit. If they come too late to be run, you may cancel their slot.

12. Participants should leave with three things: a filled out credit receipt, a signed informed consent form, and a debriefing sheet. Ask them if they have any other questions, and do your best to answer them. If you don't know the answer, you can refer them to Rachel or Rich (info at the bottom of debriefing). Make sure to thank them for their participation

13. When done for the day, lock up subject running rooms (unless someone is running subjects **immediately** after you and is already there when you leave). If you are the last subject runner of the day, please turn off the computers. Always lock up the lab when you leave unless someone else is actually in the lab.

Appendix 3

Example Consent Form

You can refer to this example of an informed consent form, taken from Kim's (2008) thesis study, when you need to generate one for your experiment.

Informed Consent Form for Biomedical Research
The Pennsylvania State University

ORP USE ONLY: IRB#21640 Doc. #1
The Pennsylvania State University
Office for Research Protections
Approval Date: 09/09/2008 – J. Mathieu
Expiration Date: 09/04/2009 – J. Mathieu
Biomedical Institutional Review Board

Title: Investigating a Forgetting Phenomenon of Knowledge and Skills

Principal Investigator: Dr. Frank E. Ritter
316G IST Bldg, University Park, PA 16802
(814) 865-4453 frank.ritter@psu.edu

Other Investigators:

Dr. Jong Wook Kim
316E IST Building
University Park, PA 16802
(814) 865-xxx; jongkim@psu.edu

Dr. Richard J. Koubek
310 Leonhard Building
University Park, PA 16802
(814) 865-xxxx rkoubek@psu.edu

1. Purpose & Description: The purpose of the study is to investigate how much knowledge and skills are forgotten and retained in human memory after a series of learning sessions. Human performance caused by forgetting will be quantitatively measured. If you decide to take part in this experiment, please follow the experimenter's instruction.

The experiment is held at 319 (Applied Cognitive Science Lab) or 205 (a computer lab) IST building. During the experiment, the timing of keystrokes and mouse movements will be recorded.

A group of participants (80 participants) selected by chance will wear an eye tracker to measure eye movements during the task, if you consent to wear the device. You can always refuse to use it. The eye tracker is a device to measure eye positions and eye movements. The eye tracker is attached to a hat, so you just can wear the hat for the experiment. The device is examined for its safety. You may be asked to talk aloud while doing the task.

2. Procedures to Be Followed: You will be asked to study an instruction booklet to learn a spreadsheet task (e.g., data normalization). Each study session will be 30 minutes maximum. For 4 days in a row, you will learn how to do the spreadsheet task.

Then you will be asked to perform the given spreadsheet tasks on a computer (duration: approximately 15 minutes).

With a retention interval of 6, 9, 12, 18, 30, or 60 days, after completing the second step, you will be asked to return to do the same spreadsheet task (duration: approximately 15 minutes/trial)

3. Voluntary Participation: The participation of this study is purely based on volunteerism. You can refuse to answer any questions. At any time, you can stop and decline the experiment. There is no penalty or loss of benefits if you refuse to participate or want to stop at any time.

4. Right to Ask Questions: You can ask questions about this research. Please contact Jong Kim at jongkim@psu.edu or 814-865-xxx with questions, complaints, concerns, or if you feel you have been harmed by this research. In addition, if you have questions about your rights as a research participant, contact the Pennsylvania State University's Office for Research Protections at (814) 865-1775.

5. Discomforts & Risks: There is no additional risk to your physical or mental health. You may experience eye fatigue because you are interacting with a computer monitor. During the experiment, you can take a break at any time.

6. Benefits: From your participation, the study is expected to obtain data representing how much knowledge and skills can be retained in the memory over time. This research can make a contribution to designing a novel training program.

7. Compensation: Participants will receive monetary compensation of $25, $30, or $35 in terms of your total trials, or extra credits (students registered to IST 331). The experiment consists of five to seven trials ($5 per trial). The compensation will be given as one lump sum after all trials. For the amount of $30 and $35, participants will receive a check issued by Penn State. Others will receive $25 cash. Total research payments within one calendar year that exceed $600 will require the University to annually report these payments to the IRS. This may require you to claim the compensation that you receive for participation in this study as taxable income.

8. Confidentiality: Your participation and data are entirely confidential. Personal identification numbers (e.g., PSU ID) will be destroyed after gathering and sorting the experimental data. Without personal identification, the gathered data will be analyzed and used for dissertation and journal publications. The following may review and copy records related to this research: The Office of Human Research Protections in the U.S. Department of Health and Human Services, the Social Science Institutional Review Board, and the PSU Office for Research Protections.

You must be 18 years of age or older to take part in this research study. If you agree to take part in this research study and the information outlined above, please sign your name and indicate the date below.

(Continued)

(Continued)

You will be given a copy of this signed and dated consent for your records.

_____   _____
Participant Signature   Date

_____   _____
Person Obtaining Consent   Date
(Principal Investigator)

Appendix 4

Example Debriefing Form

This is the debriefing form, very lightly edited, used in the study reported in Ritter, Kukreja, and St. Amant (2007).

Human–Robot Interaction Study Debriefing Form

Thank you for participating in our human–robot interface testing study.

From your participation we will learn how people use interfaces in general and human–robot interfaces in particular. These interfaces are similar to those used to work in hazardous areas, including interfaces used in rescue work at the World Trade Center. By participating, you have been able to see and use a new technology. The results can lead to improved interfaces for robots that replace humans in hazardous conditions.

You may also find the Robot project overview page useful and interesting.

If you have any questions, please feel free to ask the experimenter. You can also direct questions to Dr. Frank Ritter (frank.ritter@psu.edu, 865-4453).

Appendix 5

Example Institutional
Review Board Application

Your Institutional Review Board (IRB) will have its own review forms. These forms are based on each IRB's institutional history and the types of studies and typical problems (and atypical problems) they have had to consider over time. Thus, the form we include here can be seen only as an example form. We include it to provide you with an example of the types of questions and, more important, the types of answers characteristic of the IRB process (at least at PSU). You are responsible for the answers, but it may be useful to see how long answers are and how detailed they need to be.

Following is a form used in one of our recent studies in the lab (Paik, 2011), slightly revised to correct some errors.

Institutional Review Board (IRB)

The Office for Research Protections

205 The 330 Building

University Park, PA 16802 | 814-865-1775 |
ORProtections@psu.edu

Submitted by: Jaehyon Paik

Date Submitted: April 09, 2010 10:41:33 AM

IRB#: 33343

PI: Frank E Ritter

Study Title

1> **Study Title**

A New Training Paradigm for Knowledge and Skills Acquisition

2> **Type of eSubmission**

New

Home Department for Study

3> **Department where research is being conducted or if a student study, the department overseeing this research study.**

Industrial and Manufacturing Engineering

Review Level

4> **What level of review do you expect this research to need? NOTE: The final determination of the review level will be determined by the IRB Administrative Office. Choose from one of the following:**

Expedited

5> **Expedited Research Categories: Choose one or more of the following categories that apply to your research. You may choose more than one category but your research must meet one of the following categories to be considered for expedited review.**

Category 7—Research on individual or group characteristics or behavior (including, but not limited to, research on perception, cognition, motivation, identity, language, communication, cultural beliefs or practices, and social behavior) or research employing survey, interview, oral history, focus group, program evaluation, human factors evaluation, or quality assurance methodologies.

Basic Information: Association with Other Studies

6> Is this research study associated with other IRB-approved studies, e.g., this study is an extension study of an ongoing study or this study will use data or tissue from another ongoing study?

No

7> Where will this research study take place? Choose all that apply.

University Park

8> Specify the building, and room at University Park where this research study will take place. If not yet known, indicate as such.

The research will be held in 319 Information Sciences & Technology Building.

9> Does this research study involve any of the following centers?

None of these centers are involved in this study

10> Describe the facilities available to conduct the research for the duration of the study.

We will mainly use a computer, keyboard, mouse, and joystick to test this study. Through the computer, participants can access the specific websites that are developed by us.

11> Is this study being conducted as part of a class requirement? For additional information regarding the difference between a research study and a class requirement, see IRB Guideline IV, "Distinguishing Class-Related Pedagogical (Instructional) Assignments/Projects and Research Projects" located at http://www.research.psu.edu/orp/areas/humans/policies/guide4.asp.

No

Personnel

12> Personnel List

PSU User ID	Name	Department Affiliation	Role in this study
jzp137	Paik, Jaehyon	Industrial and Manufacturing Engineering	Co-Investigator
fer2	Frank Ritter	Information Sciences and Technology	Principal Investigator

(Continued)

(Continued)

Role in this study Principal Investigator

First Name Frank **Middle Name** E **Last Name** Ritter **Credentials** PhD
PSU User ID fer2 **E-mail Address** frank.ritter@psu.edu **PSU Employment Status** Employed
[ ] Person should receive e-mails about this application
Mailing Address 316G IST Building
Address (Line 2)
Mail Code City University Park **State** Pennsylvania **ZIP Code** 16802
Phone Number 863-xxxx **Fax number Pager Number Alternate Telephone**
Department Affiliation Information Sciences and Technology

Identify the procedures/techniques this person will perform (i.e., recruit participants, consent participants, administer the study):
This person will administer the whole process of experiments, and he will help recruit participants in his class.

Describe the person's level of experience in performing the procedures/ techniques described above:
He has lots of experience doing this kind of experiment. Most of his students who already had a PhD degree did similar experiments, from writing an IRB application to doing experiments.

Role in this study Co-Investigator

First Name Jaehyon **Middle Name Last Name** Paik **Credentials**
PSU User ID jzp137 **E-mail Address** jzp137@psu.edu **PSU Employment Status** Not Employed or Student
[X] Person should receive e-mails about this application
Mailing Address 125 Home Address Crescent
Address (Line 2)
Mail Code City State College **State** Pennsylvania **ZIP Code** 16801
Phone Number 814-876-xxxx **Fax number Pager Number Alternate Telephone**
Department Affiliation Industrial and Manufacturing Engineering

Identify the procedures/techniques this person will perform (i.e., recruit participants, consent participants, administer the study):

This person designed the entire experiment and will perform recruiting participants, receiving consent form from participants, controlling the whole process of experiments, and gathering and analyzing data from participants.

Describe the person's level of experience in performing the procedures/techniques described above:

This person is a PhD student in the IE department, and he has experience in experiments with human participants in his classes. He conducted a similar experiment during his master's studies. He also has 5 years in industry, so he has no problem designing and developing the environment.

Funding Source

13> **Is this research study funded? Funding could include the sponsor providing drugs or devices for the study. NOTE: If the study is funded or funding is pending, submit a copy of the grant proposal or statement of work for review.**

No

14> **Does this research study involve prospectively providing treatment or therapy to participants?**

No

Conflict of Interest

15> **Do any of the investigator(s), key personnel, and/or their spouses or dependent children have a financial or business interest(s) as defined by PSU Policy RA20, "Individual Conflict of Interest," associated with this research? NOTE: There is no de minimus in human participant research studies (i.e., all amounts must be reported).**

No

Purpose

16> **Provide a description of the research that includes (1) the background, (2) purpose, and (3) a description of how the research will be conducted [methodology: step-by-step process of what participants will be asked to do]. DO NOT COPY AND PASTE THE METHODOLOGY SECTION FROM THE GRANT.**

Background/Rationale: Briefly provide the background information and rationale for performing the research study.

Most research projects for exploring the effects on learning and retention by varying the training schedule have focused on two types of practice, distributed

(Continued)

(Continued)

and massed. The results indicate consistently that the distributed practice has better performance on knowledge and skills acquisition than massed practice. However, a more efficient way might exist, and I assume that a more efficient way is the hybrid practice that uses the distributed practice and massed practice together. Through this study, I will explore more efficient practice strategy.

Purpose: Summarize the study's research question(s), aims or objectives [hypothesis].

This study has two objectives, in practical and theoretical ways. The first objective is to explore the new paradigm of training strategy for tasks with declarative memory, procedural memory, and, perceptual-motor skill acquisition with different training schedules, such as distributed, hybrid 1 (massed placed in the middle of a regimen), and hybrid 2 (massed placed in the top of a regimen). And the results of each experiment are compared to verify which one is more efficient according to the task type. The second objective is to verify the results of three types of tasks with the learning and decay theories of the ACT-R cognitive architecture. The ACT-R cognitive architecture provides learning and decay theories to predict human behavior in the ACT-R model. Using these theories, I will explore to verify and summarize the results of the tasks.

Research Procedures involving Participants: Summarize the study's procedures by providing a description of how the research will be conducted [i.e., methodology—a step-by-step process of what participants will be asked to do]. Numbering each step is highly recommended. DO NOT COPY & PASTE GRANT APPLICATION IN THIS RESPONSE.

This research follows the order below: 1. Participants have overall explanation of this research (the objective of the study, which data will be gathered, and so on). 2. After explanation, participants sign a consent form. 3. Participants will have a vocabulary word test for declarative memory, tower of Hanoi game for procedural knowledge, and simple avoiding-obstacle game for perceptual motor task, and each game takes no longer than 5 minutes. 4. During the task, nothing will be asked of participants. 5. After experiments, participants will be asked not to practice the experiment until their second test.

17> **How long will participants be involved in this research study? Include the number of sessions and the duration of each session—consider the total number of minutes, hours, days, months, years, etc.**

This experiment consists of eight learning sessions and one testing session, and each session takes no longer than 20 minutes. The number of experiment days for participants varies according to the schedule type. Group 1 has 2 days, Group 2 has 8 days, and Group 3 has 4 days for the experiment.

18> **Briefly explain how you will have sufficient time to conduct and complete the research within the research period.**

On the experiment day, Jaehyon will come to the office 1 hour before the experiment to prepare the experiment, such as turning on the computer, launching the program, and launching a data correction program.

19> **List criteria for inclusion of participants:**

1. Participants should be older than 18 years. 2. Participants should have experience using a computer, keyboard, and mouse.

20> **List criteria for exclusion of participants:**

1. Participants should not have knowledge of Japanese vocabulary. 2. Participants should not have any experience with the Tower of Hanoi game.

Multi-Center Study

21> **Is this a multi-center study (i.e., study will be conducted at other institutions each with its own principal investigator)?**

No

Participant Numbers

22> **Maximum number of participants/samples/records to be enrolled by PSU investigators. NOTE: Enter one number—not a range. This number should include the estimated number that will give consent but not qualify after screening or who will otherwise withdraw and not qualify for inclusion in the final data analysis. This number should be based on a statistical analysis, unless this is a pilot study, and must match the number of participants listed in the consent form.**

30

23> **Was a statistical/power analysis conducted to determine the adequate sample size?**

Yes

Age Range of Participants

24> **Age range (check all that apply):**

18–25 years

26–40 years

(Continued)

(Continued)

Participant Information: Participant Categories

25> Choose all categories of participants who will be involved in this research study.

Healthy volunteers

26> Will Penn State students be used as study participants in this research study?

Yes

27> Will students be recruited from a Subject Pool?

No

28> Will participants be currently enrolled in a course/class of any personnel listed on this application?

Yes

29> Describe the steps taken to avoid coercion and undue influence.

We will not record any identifying information of participants, so participants can decide to participate without any coercion.

30> Will participants be employees of any personnel listed on this application?

No

31> Does this research exclude any particular gender, ethnic or racial group, and/or a person based on sexual identity?

No

32> Could some or all participants be vulnerable to coercion or undue influence due to special circumstances (do not include children, decisionally impaired, and prisoners in your answer)?

No

Recruitment

33> Describe the specific steps to be used to identify and/or contact prospective participants, records and/or tissue. If applicable, also describe how you have access to lists or records of potential participants.

We will recruit participants in two ways. The first way is that participants will be recruited from class (IST 331). We will distribute experiment flyers for participating. The second way is that participants will be recruited by posting and e-mailing lists in department or college. We will also distribute experiment flyers to the department staff, and we will ask them to distribute to students. In the experiment flyer, we describe that participants who have knowledge of Japanese vocabulary cannot participate in this experiment for screening.

34> **Will recruitment materials be used to identify potential participants?**

Yes

35> **Choose the types of recruitment materials that will be used.**

Letters/e-mails to potential participants

Script—Verbal (i.e., telephone, face-to-face, classroom)

36> **Describe how potential participants' contact information (i.e., name & address) was obtained.**

We will ask department staff to broadcast our experiment.

37> **Who will approach and/or respond to potential participants during recruitment?**

Jaehyon Paik

38> **Explain how your recruitment methods and intended population will allow you access to the required number of participants needed for this study within the proposed recruitment period.**

This experiment is not a complex task. It takes no longer than 5 minutes for each task, and it also has simple games that can be attractive to the participants.

39> **Before potential participants sign a consent document, are there any screening/eligibility questions that you need to directly ask the individual to determine whether he/she qualifies for enrollment in the study?**

Yes

40> **During screening/eligibility questions, will identifiable information about these individuals be recorded?**

No

41> **Will investigators access medical charts and/or hospital/clinic databases for recruitment purposes?**

No

42> **Will physicians/clinicians provide identifiable, patient information (e.g., name, telephone number, address) to investigators for recruitment purposes?**

No

(Continued)

(Continued)

43> Will researchers who are not involved in the care of potential participants review and/or use protected health information before a consent/authorization form is signed in the course of screening/recruiting for this research study (e.g., reviewing medical records in order to determine eligibility)?

No

Participant Consent/Assent

44> When and where will participants be approached to obtain informed consent/assent [include the timing of obtaining consent in the response]? If participants could be non-English speaking, illiterate, or have other special circumstances, describe the steps taken to minimize the possibility of coercion and undue influence.

The consent form will be given to participants on the first day in the experiment location. Participants should speak and hear English.

45> Who will be responsible for obtaining informed consent/assent from participants?

Jaehyon Paik

46> Do the people responsible for obtaining consent/assent speak the same language as the participants?

Yes

47> What type of consent/assent will be obtained? Choose all that apply.

Filled out consent form—participants will fill out and sign a consent form.

48> One of the following two conditions must be met to allow for a process other than signed informed consent to be utilized. Choose which condition is applicable. Choose only one.

The research presents no more than minimal risk of harm to participants and involves no procedures for which signed consent is normally required outside of the research context.

49> Explain how your study fits into this condition.

The experiment we will run poses no harm to the participants. We just use a computer, mouse, and keyboard—that is, this experiment may be part of everyday life.

50> If multiple groups of participants are being utilized (i.e., teachers, parents, children, people over the age of 18, others), who will and will not sign the consent/assent form? Specify for each group of participants.

Participants should read the consent form and do not need to sign because we provide implied informed consent forms.

51> Participants are to receive a copy of the informed consent form with the IRB approval stamp/statement on it. Describe how participants will receive a copy of the informed consent form to keep for their records. If this is not possible, explain why not.

The implied informed consent form states that "your participation in this research is confidential," and the form will be given to the participants before the experiment.

Cost to Participants: Compensation

52> Will the participant bear any costs which are not part of standard of care?

No

53> Will individuals be offered compensation for their participation?

Yes

Data Collection Measures/Instruments

54> Choose any of the following data collection measures/instruments that will be used in this study. Submit all instruments, measures, interview questions, and/or focus group topics/questions for review.

Knowledge/Cognitive Tests

55> Will participants be assigned to groups?

Yes

56> Will a control group(s) be used?

Yes

57> Choose one of the following:

Other control method

58> Describe the 'other' control method.

The difference variable is training schedule in this study.

Drugs/Medical Devices/
Other Substances

59> Does this research study involve the use of any of the following? Choose all that apply.

None of the above will be used in this research study

(Continued)

(Continued)

Biological Specimens

60> Will biological specimens (including blood, urine and other human-derived samples) be used in this study?

No

Recordings—Audio, Video, Digital, Photographs

61> Will any type of recordings (audio, video or digital) or photographs be made during this study?

No

Computer/Internet

62> Will any data collection for this study be conducted on the Internet or via e-mail (e.g., online surveys, observations of chat rooms or blogs, online interviews surveys via e-mail)?

No

63> Is there a method in place to authenticate the identity of the participants?

No

64> Explain why an authentication method is not in place to identify respondents.

We do not collect identifying information of participants.

65> Will data be sent in an encrypted format?

No

66> Explain why the data will not be sent in an encrypted format.

We do not record identifying information of participants.

67> Will a commercial service provider (i.e., SurveyMonkey, Psych Data, Zoomerang) be used to collect data or for data storage?

No

Risks: Potential for and Seriousness of

68> List the potential discomforts and risks (physical, psychological, legal, social, or financial) AND describe the likelihood or seriousness of the discomforts/risks. For studies presenting no more than minimal risk, loss of confidentiality may be the main risk associated with the research.

Memorizing the Japanese vocabulary may cause discomfort to participants.

69> Describe how the discomforts and risks will be minimized and/or how participants will be protected against potential discomforts/risks throughout the study (e.g., label research data/specimens with code numbers, screening to assure appropriate selection of participants, identify standard of care procedures, sound research design, safety monitoring and reporting).

We assume that there is no risk in this experiment. However, if participants feel discomfort in the experiment, they can quit immediately and can reschedule or give up the experiment.

70> Does this research involve greater than minimal risk to the participants?

No

Benefits to Participants

71> What are the potential benefits to the individual participants of the proposed research study? (If none, state "None.") NOTE: Compensation cannot be considered a benefit.

None

72> What are the potential benefits to others from the proposed research study?

The result may show the needs of new training paradigm.

Deception

73> Does this study involve giving false or misleading information to participants or withholding information from them such that their "informed" consent is in question?

No

Confidentiality

74> Describe the provisions made to maintain confidentiality of the data, including medical records and specimens. Choose all that apply.

Locked offices

75> Describe the provisions made to protect the privacy interests of the participants and minimize intrusion.

First of all, we do not store any private information of participants, and the collected data will be stored in a locked office. Only the experimenter, Jaehyon Paik, can access the data.

(Continued)

(Continued)

76> Will the study data and/or specimens contain identifiable information?

No

77> Who will have access to the study data and/or specimens?

Jaehyon Paik (only)

78> Will identifiers be disclosed to a sponsor or collaborators at another institution?

No

79> Will a record or list containing a code (i.e., code number, pseudonym) and participants' identity be used in this study?

No

80> What will happen to the data when the research has been completed? Choose one.

Stored for length of time required by federal regulations/funding source and then destroyed [minimum of 3 years]

81> Is information being collected for this research that could have adverse consequences for participants or damage their financial standing, employability, insurability or reputation?

No

82> Will a "Certificate of Confidentiality" be obtained from the federal government?

No

HIPAA (Health Insurance Portability and Accountability Act)

83> Will participants' protected health information (PHI) be obtained for this study?

No

Radiation

84> Will any participants be asked to undergo a diagnostic radiation procedure while enrolled in this study?

No

Physical Activity

85> Will participants be required to engage in or perform any form of physical activity?

No

86> Will any type of electrical equipment other than audio headphones be attached to the participants (e.g., EMG, EKG, special glasses)? Submit a letter regarding the most recent safety check of the x-ray equipment being used with the supporting documents for this application.

No

Document Upload

ICFS   Document 1001 Received 03/22/2010 11:19:22 - Adult Form Revised version of consent form

INSTRUMENTS   Document 1001 Received 03/22/2010 11:47:14 - For data collection - All data are recorded in webpage   Document 1002 Received 04/09/2010 10:37:36 - The screenshots for the tasks. Document 1003 Received 04/09/2010 10:38:13 - Task2   Document 1004 Received 04/09/2010 10:38:51 - task3

RECRUITMENT   Document 1001 Received 03/22/2010 11:20:24 - Recruitment Material Revised version of recruitment mat   Document 1002 Received 04/09/2010 10:16:47 - Eligibility Screening This document for Eligibility Scr

SUBMISSION FORMS   Document 1001 Received 03/23/2010 09:04:42 AM - Application Auto-generated by eSubmission Approval

- Click ADD to upload a new document for review
- Click REPLACE to upload a revised version of a previously submitted document (the radio button next to the document to be revised must be selected before clicking replace)
- Click REMOVE to delete a document. NOTE: Documents can be deleted at any time prior to submission. If an eSubmission is returned for additional information, only new uploaded documents can be deleted.
- To view a document just click on the document name. The following file types can be uploaded: .doc, .docx, .xls, .xlsx, .ppt, .pptx, .pub, .tif, .tif, .tiff, .txt, .pdf, .rtf, .jpg, .gif

Appendix 6

Considerations When Running a Study Online

Many studies are now moving "online"—that is, the subjects are interacting with experiments that are run online through a web browser (the Social Psychology Network provides a list of such studies at www.socialpsychology.org/expts.htm). Using online studies, when properly done, has the ability to greatly increase your sample size, and these studies certainly offer the possibility of a much more diverse sample. You can, however, lose experimental control (you won't actually know who is participating in many circumstances), and some technical sophistication may be required to create and use an online study.

Online studies have some special considerations. This section notes a few considerations to keep in mind when running these studies. This section does not consider the choice of tools to run a study, such as Amazon's Mechanical Turk or commercial tools to create surveys, because the book focuses on how to start running studies, not how to design, implement, or analyze them, per se. This appendix is also not complete because online surveys is a growing area, and this appendix is designed only to introduce you to some of the issues in this area. For more complete treatments, see the references in the "Further Readings" section.

A6.1 Recruiting Subjects

If you are recruiting subjects to participate in a study, you might choose to go online to recruit them. If you do so, keep in mind that the request should be fair, and if your study is under an Institutional Review Board (IRB), how you recruit must go through the IRB as well.

There is a delicate balance to sharing information and drawing attention to opportunities appropriately that most people understand in the real world, but we are still learning about in the online world. We have argued previously (Cheyne & Ritter, 2001) that you should not recruit subjects through unsolicited direct e-mail, although our university does this to distraction at times. For example, it seems inappropriate to send announcements about competitions to create "learning badges" to "professors at universities we could find," as a private university in Durham, North Carolina, recently did.

Putting the flyer (or announcement) on a very relevant mailing list can be acceptable if such a mailing list is available and appropriate. Posting announcements of studies on related websites can also be very appropriate. It may also be advisable, and perhaps overlooked, to disseminate study announcements for online studies through the same channels you would use for a non-online study, such as flyers and class announcements. But, it is very inappropriate to send such materials where there is little chance of finding suitable subjects or where the subjects being recruited are reluctant to participate. Take advice if you have doubts.

If your subjects are recruited in such a way that you don't see them, you might wish to take a few more demographic measures, depending on your theory and the hypothesis—for example, what countries subjects are in (if your software can't tell from the IP addresses of their machines) or level of education and first language. One of the clearest summaries of this problem was noted in Lock Haven University's student newspaper (October 14, 2010, p. A7) about their online poll:

> This . . . poll is not scientific and reflects the opinions of only those Internet users who have chosen to participate. The results cannot be assumed to represent the opinions of Internet users in general, nor the public as a whole.

If you can work around this restriction—for example, finding best performance or examples—then your results will be worthwhile. If you gather the results as representative, then you are subject to this restriction.

If the link to your software has been widely disseminated, you should have the software fail gracefully after the study is done. For example, if your survey is no longer up on your web server, you could put a page up noting this and thanking those who have participated.

A6.2 Apparatus

Because the apparatus for gathering the data will be automatic and you will not be able to answer questions that arise (in most cases), the interaction needs to be particularly clear and correct. So you should run more extensive pilot studies than you would for other studies, examine the interaction experience yourself, and have the principal investigator and other research assistants use the apparatus to make sure there are no typos, unclear wordings, or other potential problems. You should also back up information from the server you are using to another machine daily.

If your apparatus is taking timing information, you should test this and not take it for granted. A timer that reports user interaction times with millisecond precision doesn't necessarily generate time stamps that are accurate to a millisecond. This can be difficult to test, but before you report timing data, you should attempt to measure its accuracy.

A6.3 Gaming Your Apparatus

You should check your data daily. This will help you tell how subject recruitment is going. It will also help you see if a person or group is gaming the experiment. Subjects might be doing it multiple times because it is fun (but this might not provide useful data or might slow down your server), or they might enjoy "messing up" your experiment. If you find anomalies, you should contact your principal investigator with these concerns. You should also talk about criteria for removing data you believe are not provided in earnest.

A6.4 Further Readings

Kraut, R., Olson, J., Banaji, M., Bruckman, A., Cohen, J., & Couper, M. (2004). Psychological research online: Report of Board of Scientific Affairs' Advisory Group on the Conduct of Research on the Internet. *American Psychologist, 59*(2), 105–117.

Yeager, D. S., Krosnick, J. A., Chang, L., Javitz, H. S., Levendusky, M. S., Simpser, A., et al. (2011). Comparing the accuracy of RDD telephone surveys and Internet surveys conducted with probability and non-probability samples. *Public Opinion Quarterly, 75*, 709–747.

These papers by Kraut et al. and Yeager et al., available online, describe some of the theoretical differences between real-world and Internet studies, and online and telephone surveys, including the need to understand who your respondents are.

Joinson, A., McKenna, K., Postmes, T., & Reips, U.-D. (2007). *Oxford handbook of Internet psychology*. New York: Oxford University Press.

This book includes a section (eight chapters) on doing research on the Internet.

References

Al-Harkan, I. M., & Ramadan, M. Z. (2005). Effects of pixel shape and color, and matrix pixel density of Arabic digital typeface on characters' legibility. *International Journal of Industrial Ergonomics, 35*(7), 652–664.

American Federation for the Blind. (2012, January). *Interpreting Bureau of Labor Statistics employment data.* Retrieved from http://www.afb.org/Section.asp?SectionID=15&SubTopicID=177

American Psychological Association. (2010). *Publication manual of the American Psychological Association* (6th ed.). New York: Author.

Anderson, J. R., Bothell, D., & Douglass, S. (2004). Eye movements do not reflect retrieval processes. *Psychological Science, 15*(4), 225–231.

Avraamides, M., & Ritter, F. E. (2002). Using multidisciplinary expert evaluations to test and improve cognitive model interfaces. In *Proceedings of the 11th Computer Generated Forces Conference* (pp. 553–562). Orlando: University of Central Florida.

Bethel, C. L., & Murphy, R. M. (2010). Review of human studies methods in HRI and recommendations. *International Journal of Social Robotics, 2,* 347–359.

Bloom, B. D. (1984). The 2 sigma problem: The search for methods of group instruction as effective as one-to-one tutoring. *Educational Researcher, 13,* 3–16.

Boehm, B., & Hansen, W. (2001). The Spiral Model as a tool for evolutionary acquisition. *Crosstalk: The Journal of Defense Software Engineering, 14*(5), 4–11.

Brown, S., & Heathcote, A. (2003). Averaging learning curves across and within participants. *Behavior Research Methods, Instruments and Computers, 35,* 11–21.

Bryan, W. L., & Harter, N. (1897). Studies in the physiology and psychology of the telegraphic language. *Psychological Review, 4,* 27–53.

Campbell, D. T., & Stanley, J. C. (1963). *Experimental and quasi-experimental designs for research.* Boston: Houghton Mifflin.

Carlson, R. A., Avraamides, M. N., Cary, M., & Strasberg, S. (2007). What do the hands externalize in simple arithmetic? *Journal of Experimental Psychology: Learning, Memory, and Cognition, 33,* 747–756.

Carlson, R. A., & Cassenti, D. N. (2004). Intentional control of event counting. *Journal of Experimental Psychology: Learning, Memory, and Cognition, 30,* 1235–1251.

Carroll, J. M. (Ed.). (2000). *HCI models, theories, and frameworks: Toward a multidisciplinary science.* Burlington, MA: Morgan-Kauffmann.

Cassavaugh, N. D., & Kramer, A. F. (2009). Transfer of computer-based training to simulated driving in older adults. *Applied Ergonomics, 40,* 943–952.

Cheyne, T., & Ritter, F. E. (2001). Targeting respondents on the Internet successfully and responsibly. *Communications of the ACM, 44*(4), 94–98.

Cohen, J. (1988). *Statistical power analysis for the behavioral sciences* (2nd ed.). Hillsdale, NJ: Lawrence Erlbaum.

Cohen, J. (1992). A power primer. *Psychological Bulletin, 112,* 155–159.

Cozby, P. C. (2004). *Methods in behavioral research* (8th ed.). New York: McGraw-Hill.

Crossman, E. R. F. W. (1959). A theory of the acquisition of speed-skill. *Ergonomics, 2,* 153–166.

Darley, J. M., Zanna, M. P., & Roediger, H. L. (Eds.). (2003). *The compleat academic: A practical guide for the beginning social scientist* (2nd ed.). Washington, DC: American Psychological Association.

de Groot, A. D., & Gobet, F. (1996). *Perception and memory in chess.* Assen, Netherlands: Van Gorcum.

Delaney, P. F., Reder, L. M., Staszewski, J. J., & Ritter, F. E. (1998). The strategy specific nature of improvement: The power law applies by strategy within task. *Psychological Science, 9*(1), 1–8.

Dhami, M. K., & Hertwig, R. (2004). The role of representative design in an ecological approach to cognition. *Psychological Bulletin, 130,* 959–988.

Digiusto, E. (1994). Equity in authorship: A strategy for assigning credit when publishing. *Social Science & Medicine, 38*(1), 55–58.

Ebbinghaus, H. (1964). *Memory: A contribution to experimental psychology.* New York: Dover. (Original work published 1885)

Ericsson, K. A., & Simon, H. A. (1980). Protocol analysis: Verbal reports as data. *Psychological Review, 87,* 215–251.

Ericsson, K. A., & Simon, H. A. (1993). *Protocol analysis: Verbal reports as data* (2nd ed.). Cambridge, MA: MIT Press.

Estes, W. K. (1956). The problem of inference from group data. *Psychological Bulletin, 53,* 134–140.

Fishman, G. A. (2003). When your eyes have a wet nose: The evolution of the use of guide dogs and establishing the seeing eye. *Survey of Ophthalmology, 48*(4), 452–458.

Fitts, P. M. (1954). The information capacity of the human motor system in controlling amplitude of movement. *Journal of Experimental Psychology, 47*(6), 381–391.

Friedrich, M. B. (2008). *Implementierung von schematischen Denkstrategien in einer höheren Programmiersprache: Erweitern und Testen der vorhandenen Resultate durch Erfassen von zusätzlichen Daten und das Erstellen von weiteren Strategien*

[*Implementing diagrammatic reasoning strategies in a high level language: Extending and testing the existing model results by gathering additional data and creating additional strategies*]. Faculty of Information Systems and Applied Computer Science, University of Bamberg, Germany.

Hart, S. G., & Staveland, L. E. (1988). Development of the NASA-TLX (Task Load Index): Results of empirical and theoretical research. In P. A. Hancock & N. Meshkati (Eds.), *Human mental workload* (pp. 139–185). Amsterdam: North Holland.

Heathcote, A., Brown, S., & Mewhort, D. J. K. (2000). Repealing the power law: The case for an exponential law of practice. *Psychonomic Bulletin & Review, 7,* 185–207.

Hill, E. W., & Ponder, P. (1976). *Orientation and mobility techniques: A guide for the practitioner.* New York: American Foundation for the Blind.

Howell, D. C. (2008). *Fundamental statistics for the behavioral sciences* (6th ed.). Belmont, CA: Thompson Wadsworth.

Jonassen, D. H., & Grabowski, B. L. (1993). *Handbook of individual differences, learning, and instruction.* Hillsdale, NJ: Erlbaum.

Jones, G., Ritter, F. E., & Wood, D. J. (2000). Using a cognitive architecture to examine what develops. *Psychological Science, 11*(2), 93–100.

Kennedy, S. (1989). Using video in the BNR usability lab. *SIGCHI Bulletin, 21*(2), 92–95.

Keppel, G., & Wickens, T. D. (2004). *Design and analysis: A researcher's handbook.* Upper Saddle River, NJ: Prentice Hall/Pearson Education.

Kim, D. S., Emerson, R. W., & Curtis, A. (2009). Drop-off detection with the long cane: Effects of different cane techniques on performance. *Journal of Visual Impairment & Blindness, 103*(9), 519–530.

Kim, J. W. (2008). *Procedural skills: From learning to forgetting.* Unpublished doctoral dissertation, Department of Industrial and Manufacturing Engineering, The Pennsylvania State University, University Park, PA.

Kim, J. W., Koubek, R. J., & Ritter, F. E. (2007). Investigation of procedural skills degradation from different modalities. In *Proceedings of the 8th International Conference on Cognitive Modeling* (pp. 255–260). Oxford, UK: Taylor & Francis/Psychology Press.

Kim, J. W., & Ritter, F. E. (2007). Automatically recording keystrokes in public clusters with RUI: Issues and sample answers. In *Proceedings of the 29th Annual Cognitive Science Society* (p. 1787). Austin, TX: Cognitive Science Society.

Kirlik, A. (2010). Brunswikian theory and method as a foundation for simulation-based research on clinical judgment. *Simulation in Healthcare, 5*(5), 255–259.

Kukreja, U., Stevenson, W. E., & Ritter, F. E. (2006). RUI: Recording user input from interfaces under Window and Mac OS X. *Behavior Research Methods, 38*(4), 656–659.

Lintern, G., Sheppard, D. J., Parker, D. L., Yates, K. E., & Nolan, M. D. (1989). Simulator design and instructional features for air-to-ground attack: A transfer study. *Human Factors, 31,* 87–99.

Mackay, W. E. (1995). Ethics, lies and videotape. In *Proceedings of ACM CHI '95 Human Factors in Computing Systems* (pp. 138–145). Denver, CO: ACM Press.

MacWhinney, B., St. James, J., Schunn, C., Li, P., & Schneider, W. (2001). STEP—A system for teaching experimental psychology using E-Prime. *Behavioral Research Methods, Instruments, & Computers, 33*(2), 287–296.

Mané, A. M., & Donchin, E. (1989). The Space Fortress game. *Acta Psychologica, 71,* 17–22.

Marron, J. A., & Bailey, I. L. (1982). Visual factors and orientation-mobility performance. *American Journal of Optometry and Physiological Optics, 59*(5), 413–426.

Masson, M. E. J., & Loftus, G. R. (2003). Using confidence intervals for graphically based data interpretation. *Canadian Journal of Experimental Psychology, 57,* 203–220.

Mitchell, M. L., & Jolley, J. M. (2012). *Research design explained* (8th ed.). Belmont, CA: Wadsworth.

Montgomery, D. C. (2001). *Design and analysis of experiments* (5th ed.). New York: John Wiley & Sons.

Moon, J., Bothell, D., & Anderson, J. R. (2011). Using a cognitive model to provide instruction for a dynamic task. In *Proceedings of the 33rd Annual Conference of the Cognitive Science Society* (pp. 2283–2288). Austin, TX: Cognitive Science Society.

Morgan, J. H., Cheng, C.-Y., Pike, C., & Ritter, F. E. (in press). A design, tests, and considerations for improving keystroke and mouse loggers. *Interacting with Computers.*

Munro, G. D. (2011). Falling on deaf ears. *The Psychologist, 24*(3), 178–181. Retrieved from http://www.thepsychologist.org.uk/archive/archive_home.cfm/volumeID_24-editionID_198-ArticleID_1806-getfile_getPDF/thepsychologist/0311munro.pdf

Murphy, R. R., Blitch, J., & Casper, J. (2002). AAAI/RoboCup-2001 Urban Search and Rescue Events: Reality and competition. *AI Magazine, 23*(1), 37–42.

NASA. (1987). *NASA Task Load Index (NASA-TLX) Version 1.0: Computerized version.* Moffett Field, CA: Human Performance Research Group, NASA Ames Research Center. Retrieved from http://humansystems.arc.nasa.gov/groups/TLX/downloads/TLX_comp_manual.pdf

Nerb, J., Spada, H., & Ernst, A. M. (1997). A cognitive model of agents in a commons dilemma. In *Proceedings of the 19th Annual Conference of the Cognitive Science Society* (pp. 560–565). Mahwah, NJ: Erlbaum.

Newell, A., & Simon, H. A. (1972). *Human problem solving.* Englewood Cliffs, NJ: Prentice Hall.

Nielsen, J. (1994). Usability laboratories. *Behaviour & Information Technology, 13*(1–2), 3–8.

Nielsen, J., & Molich, R. (1990). Heuristic evaluation of user interfaces. In *Proceedings of CHI '90* (pp. 249–256). New York: ACM.

Ohlsson, S. (1992). Artificial instruction: A method for relating learning theory to instructional design. In M. Jones & P. H. Winne (Eds.), *Adaptive learning environments: Foundations and frontiers* (pp. 55–83). Berlin: Springer-Verlag.

Orne, M. T., & Whitehouse, W. G. (2000). Demand characteristics. In A. E. Kazdin (Ed.), *Encyclopedia of psychology* (pp. 469–470). Washington, DC: American Psychological Association and Oxford University Press.

Paik, J. (2011). *A novel training paradigm for knowledge and skills acquisition: Hybrid schedules lead to better learning for some but not all tasks.* Unpublished doctoral thesis, Industrial Engineering, The Pennsylvania State University, University Park, PA.

Payne, J. W., Braunstein, M. L., & Carroll, J. S. (1978). Exploring predecisional behavior: An alternative approach to decision research. *Organizational Behavior and Human Performance, 22,* 17–44.

Pew, R. W., & Mavor, A. S. (Eds.). (2007). *Human-system integration in the system development process: A new look.* Washington, DC: National Academy Press. Retrieved from http://books.nap.edu/catalog.php?record_id=11893

Proctor, R. W., & Dutta, A. (1995). *Skill acquisition and human performance.* Thousand Oaks, CA: Sage.

Ray, W. J. (2003). *Methods: Toward a science of behavior and experience* (7th ed.). Belmont, CA: Wadsworth/Thompson Learning.

Reder, L. M., & Ritter, F. E. (1988). Feeling of knowing and strategy selection for solving arithmetic problems. *Bulletin of the Psychonomic Society, 26*(6), 495–496.

Reder, L. M., & Ritter, F. E. (1992). What determines initial feeling of knowing? Familiarity with question terms, not the answer. *Journal of Experimental Psychology: Learning, Memory & Cognition, 18*(3), 435–451.

Rempel, D., Willms, K., Anshel, J., Jaschinski, W., & Sheedy, J. (2007). The effects of visual display distance on eye accommodation, head posture, and vision and neck symptoms. *Human Factors, 49*(5), 830–838.

Ritter, F. E. (1989). *The effect of feature frequency on feeling-of-knowing and strategy selection for arithmetic problems.* Unpublished master's thesis, Department of Psychology, Carnegie Mellon University, Pittsburgh, PA.

Ritter, F. E., Baxter, G. D., & Churchill, E. F. (in press). *The basics of human-system interaction: What system designers really need to know about people.* New York: Springer.

Ritter, F. E., Kim, J. W., Morgan, J. H., & Carlson, R. A. (2011). Practical aspects of running experiments with human participants. In *Universal Access in HCI, Part I, HCII 2011, LNCS 6765* (pp. 119–128). Berlin: Springer-Verlag.

Ritter, F. E., Kukreja, U., & St. Amant, R. (2007). Including a model of visual processing with a cognitive architecture to model a simple teleoperation task. *Journal of Cognitive Engineering and Decision Making, 1*(2), 121–147.

Ritter, F. E., & Larkin, J. H. (1994). Developing process models as summaries of HCI action sequences. *Human-Computer Interaction, 9,* 345–383.

Ritter, F. E., Schoelles, M. J., Quigley, K. S., & Klein, L. C. (2011). Determining the number of model runs: Treating cognitive models as theories by not sampling their behavior. In L. Rothrock & S. Narayanan (Eds.), *Human-in-the-loop simulations: Methods and practice* (pp. 97–116). London: Springer-Verlag.

Ritter, F. E., & Schooler, L. J. (2001). The learning curve. In W. Kintch, N. Smelser, & P. Baltes (Eds.), *International encyclopedia of the social and behavioral sciences* (Vol. 13, pp. 8602–8605). Amsterdam: Pergamon.

Roediger, H. (2004). What should they be called? *APS Observer, 17*(4), 46–48.

Rosenbloom, P. S., & Newell, A. (1987). Learning by chunking, a production system model of practice. In D. Klahr, P. Langley, & R. Neches (Eds.), *Production system models of learning and development* (pp. 221–286). Cambridge, MA: MIT Press.

Rosson, M. B., & Carroll, J. M. (2002). *Usability engineering: Scenario-based development of human–computer interaction.* San Francisco: Morgan Kaufmann.

Salvucci, D. D. (2001). An integrated model of eye movements and visual encoding. *Cognitive Systems Research, 1*(4), 201–220.

Salvucci, D. D. (2009). Rapid prototyping and evaluation of in-vehicle interfaces. *ACM Transactions on Computer–Human Interaction, 16*(2), Article 9, 33 pages.

Salvucci, D. D., & Goldberg, J. H. (2000). Identifying fixations and saccades in eye-tracking protocols. In *Proceedings of the Eye Tracking Research and Applications Symposium* (pp. 71–78). New York: ACM Press.

Sanderson, P. M., & Fisher, C. A. (1994). Exploratory sequential data analysis: Foundations. *Human-Computer Interaction, 9*(3–4), 251–317.

Schoelles, M. J., & Gray, W. D. (2000). Argus Prime: Modeling emergent microstrategies in a complex simulated task environment. In *Proceedings of the 3rd International Conference on Cognitive Modeling* (pp. 260–270). Veenendaal, Netherlands: Universal Press.

Schoelles, M. J., & Gray, W. D. (2001). Argus: A suite of tools for research in complex cognition. *Behavior Research Methods, Instruments, & Computers, 33*(2), 130–140.

Schooler, J. W., Ohlsson, S., & Brooks, K. (1993). Thoughts beyond words: When language overshadows insight. *Journal of Experimental Psychology: General, 122*, 166–183.

Seibel, R. (1963). Discrimination reaction time for a 1,023-alternative task. *Journal of Experimental Psychology, 66*(3), 215–226.

Siegler, R. S. (1987). The perils of averaging data over strategies: An example from children's addition. *Journal of Experimental Psychology, 115*, 250–264.

Smallman, H. S., & St. John, M. (2005). Naïve Realism: Misplaced faith in the utility of realistic displays. *Ergonomics in Design, 13*(3/Summer), 6–13.

Sweeney, L. (2000). Foundations of privacy protection from a computer science perspective. In *Proceedings, Joint Statistical Meeting.* Indianapolis, IN: American Association for the Advancement of Science.

Tuckman, H. P., & Leahey, J. (1975). What is an article worth? *Journal of Political Economy, 83*(5), 951–967.

VanLehn, K. (2007). Getting out of order: Avoiding lesson effects through instruction In F. E. Ritter, J. Nerb, T. O'Shea, & E. Lehtinen (Eds.), *In order to learn: How the sequences of topics affect learning* (pp. 169–179). New York: Oxford University Press.

Wagenmakers, E., & Grünwald, P. (2006). A Bayesian perspective on hypothesis testing: A comment on Killeen (2005). *Psychological Science, 17,* 641–642.

Wilkinson, L. (1999). Statistical methods in psychology journals: Guidelines and explanations. *American Psychologist, 54,* 594–604.

Winston, A. S. (1990). Robert Sessions Woodworth and the "Columbia Bible": How the psychological experiment was redefined. *American Journal of Psychology, 103*(3), 391–401.

Wisconsin Department of Health Services. (2006). *Sighted guide techniques.* Madison, WI: Author. Retrieved from http://www.dhs.wisconsin.gov/blind/adjustment/sightedguide.pdf

Woodworth, R. S. (1938). *Experimental psychology.* Oxford, UK: Holt.

Yeh, K.-C., Gregory, J. P., & Ritter, F. E. (2010). One Laptop per Child: Polishing up the XO Laptop user experience. *Ergonomics in Design, 18*(3), 8–13.

Index

Note: n in locator refers to the footnote number.

⊛SAGE research**methods**

The essential online tool for researchers from the world's leading methods publisher

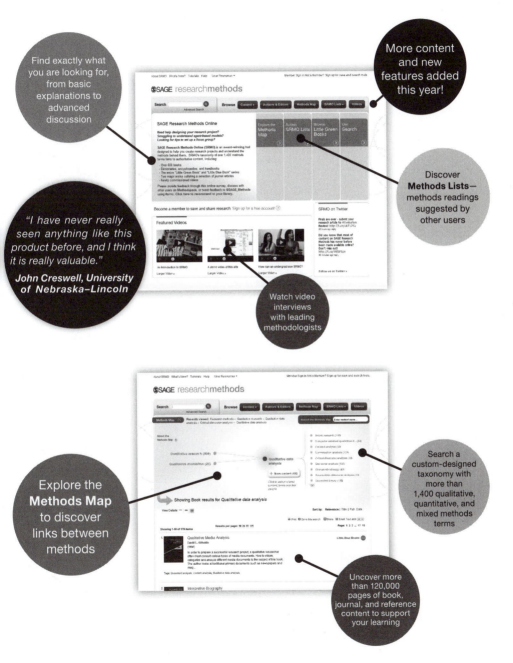

Find exactly what you are looking for, from basic explanations to advanced discussion

More content and new features added this year!

"I have never really seen anything like this product before, and I think it is really valuable."

John Creswell, University of Nebraska–Lincoln

Discover **Methods Lists**— methods readings suggested by other users

Watch video interviews with leading methodologists

Explore the **Methods Map** to discover links between methods

Search a custom-designed taxonomy with more than 1,400 qualitative, quantitative, and mixed methods terms

Uncover more than 120,000 pages of book, journal, and reference content to support your learning

Find out more at
www.sageresearchmethods.com